"Some men see things as they are and ask why. Others dream things that never were and ask why not."
— George Bernard Shaw

"The reasonable man adapts himself to the world, the unreasonable one persists in trying to adapt the world to himself. Therefore, all progress depends on the unreasonable man. ...

"Being unreasonable is not just a state of mind. It is also a process by which older, outdated forms of reasoning are jettisoned and new ones conceived and evolved. As the process unfolds, those mired in the older, obsolete paradigms can become threatened by—and aggressive toward—the innovators, particularly if those innovators move into the mainstream worlds of business, finance, and politics. But like it or not, the world is in the early stages of powerful, deep-running, and pervasive changes that, for better or worse, will transform its economies, its cultures, and people's understanding of who they are and what they stand for."[1]

---

[1] George Bernard Shaw, "Man and Superman: Maxims for Revolutionaries" 1903, in *Plays by George Bernard Shaw*, New York: Penguin.

**You Snooze ... You Lose:
Thriving in These Turbulent Times!**

Copyright © 2010 Jerry Twombly
All rights reserved, including the right to reproduce this book or portions thereof in any form whatsoever.

ISBN: 9781095015704

This book is dedicated to Dan and Claudia Cook, Joe and Karen Morello, Scot and Debi Robinson, and my beloved wife Sue, partners together in the pursuit of opportunities to impact our world through The Service Station[2] ... *a center for serving communities worldwide.*

---

[2] www.theservicestation.org

Special thanks to David Andersen for his excellent work on the cover of this book.

And thanks to Ghostwriter, Author and Editor Dwight Clough for his assistance with this manuscript. Dwight specializes in Christian inspirational, biographical and related books. Learn more at DwightClough.com.

Table of Contents

Preface	7
Introduction	10
Prologue	15
1 The New Economy	18
2 What in the World Happened?	25
3 The Heart of the Matter	33
4 The Outsource Rage	43
5 Changing Attitudes	51
6 The Need for Partnerships	58
7 Bigger Isn't Better	69
8 Mergers and Strategic Alliances	74
9 Some Things Never Change	81
10 The Turning Point	88
11 New Economy Thinking	93
12 Strategic Planning	98

13 Marketing, Sales and Rebrands	107
14 Painless Giving	118
15 The Elephant in the Room	126
16 Winners and Losers	131
Conclusion: You Snooze, You Lose	143
Appendix: Nine Tsunamis that Will Rock Our World	145
Resources	150

"At the end of the day, an organization's success will be ultimately measured in terms of how successful they have been in building relationships."

Preface

Success is measured in relationships. Without relationships, businesses crash and nonprofits fail. But, when we build meaningful and sustainable friendships and alliances, organizations thrive. This was the message of my book, **Funding Your Vision: New Hope for nonprofits.** From the beginning, the book captured the imaginations of an entire generation of nonprofit leaders and moved many to establish strong development programs that have yielded multiplied millions of dollars.

But then, something happened.

When two planes flew into the twin towers of The World Trade Center on September 11th, 2001, our nation changed. Overnight, terrorism became the new reality. The "war on terror" converged with the most catastrophic economic upheaval in 70 years. In the wake of this political and financial uncertainty, organizations of every type struggle to survive.

Some use the term "economic crisis" to identify the chaos surrounding this new reality. I would like to suggest that the world wide economic crisis is now the *New Economy*.

Our world has changed. Permanently. And while the principles of relational development introduced in **Funding Your Vision** have not changed, the application of them is taking on a totally new look in the New Economy.

Change is inevitable. Organizations that fail to adapt to the new realities will quickly lose their place in a changing world. We must adapt, and we must do it now. If we snooze, we lose. Those who fall asleep at the helm in hopes that they will wake up in the morning and find things back as they were will lose. They may continue as relics, solemn reminders of the days gone by, or, more likely, they may be lost forever. The world of 2020 and beyond will bear little resemblance to the world at the beginning of the century. Nonprofits will be leaner, more productive, and many will become self-sustaining. The entrepreneurial spirit will be reborn, extravagant practices will diminish, and a conservative pragmatism will take its place.

For the last several years I have been talking about

this with groups, organizations, forums, and with our clients around the world. I wanted to write about it and hence this volume, *You Snooze, You Lose: Adapting to the New Economy*.

In *Funding Your Vision*, I told the story of a Frustrated Man who tried to make sense of an age long dilemma: How can individuals who respect and admire a nonprofit, be indifferent about its success? Along the way he met a Visionary who helped him grasp the core principles of relational development.

Readers grew to relate to the Frustrated Man. And since it seems that the New Economy has birthed again frustration and anxiety, it seemed to me appropriate to bring our two "friends" back together again for a prolonged discussion of the New Economy.

I hope you enjoy this book. Even more, I am hopeful that you will choose to view your life and work through the lens of this new reality. I hope you will gain insight, understanding, and new perspectives that will enable your organization to fulfill its mission more effectively and that God might grant you the courage to change and be a leading force in the New Economy.

Jerry Twombly
September, 2010

"Difficulty has always been the precursor to change, change that might have otherwise never occurred. Medicines were developed to bring relief to those who suffered... Need and the accompanying pain it brings has been the mother of creativity and the root of personal character."

Introduction

The Visionary sat alone in a corner chair at the local coffee café pondering the papers before him. The morning on-their-way-to-work crowd gathered around the barista to place their orders. They hastily checked email on iPhones while they waited for their morning brew.

But the Visionary was oblivious to those around him. He re-read the first draft of an article he had been commissioned to write on the topic "The Entitlement Dilemma." The views he had expressed for years were now beginning to resonate with others, and he wanted to say them well. He paused to reread a portion of his first draft.

"Ever since the presidential administration of Franklin Roosevelt things dramatically changed

in the United States. The economic trauma caused by the Great Depression had impacted millions and a wide new range of plans were introduced designed to stabilize the economy and get people back to work.

"And while many of the changes made during this era were effective in addressing short-term goals, they also created an unusual financial burden upon government to sustain them."

His highlight pen in hand, the Visionary wanted to make sure his statements were not perceived as politically motivated. Still wondering if the logical sequence made sense, he continued to read:

"Entitlements, obligations the government is committed to meet under law, now make up nearly 70% of the budget of the United States of America. And while many clearly benefit by entitlement programs and justifiably depend on them, the underlying collateral damage done has been attitudinal; the idea that somehow someone else is responsible for their well-being."

He lifted his head. This was the point he wanted to make. His purpose was to uncover an underlying paradigm that permeates both the public and private sectors. Looking to others for help rather than seizing challenges and overcoming them seemed to characterize a nearly universal mindset.

He searched through his notes and found another paragraph:

> "Difficulty has always been the precursor to change, change that might have otherwise never occurred. Medicines were developed to bring relief to those who suffered; technological innovations were created to enhance productivity. Need and the accompanying pain it brings has been the mother of creativity and the root of personal character.
>
> "In authoritarian communism, the state took over the responsibilities that should belong to individuals, and robbed much of the earth's population of the motivation to reach beyond themselves and created a dependency on the state that robbed millions of personal initiative and creativity.
>
> "Pain is good and an important part of life. Wise parents allow their children to experience difficulty and don't always try to fix things. Their hope is that they will look to themselves for answers and not to someone to rescue them. Bailing out anyone who struggles is not always the best answer, in fact it can be counter-productive."

The Visionary thought back to a conversation he had participated in earlier that month among a group of nonprofit leaders. They spoke of the impact the economic crisis was having on their organizations and were discussing ways to increase donor income. He listened to the discussion and found himself becoming increasingly uncomfortable with the direction it was taking. He sensed something was wrong.

From that conversation thoughts began to crystallize in his mind. Many of the nonprofit leaders with whom he worked had developed an attitude that their primary problem was money. There seemed to be a prevailing attitude that if you throw enough money at a problem it will disappear. These were the thoughts that led to the article he was writing.

The Visionary picked up his pen and scribbled a few more notes.

> *"Throwing good money at a bad idea alienates those who want to make a difference with their dollars.*
>
> *"Nonprofits, in turmoil because of depleting resources, hope this problem will soon go away. But it will not. Revenues are not likely to return to prior levels, at least not in the short term.*
>
> *"The paradigms upon which many organizations are built were shaky in a good economy, and are proving impossible to sustain in a bad one.*
>
> *"Everyone is looking for instant relief. But whatever happened to responsibility? What happened*

> to the can-do spirit that inspired and empowered previous generations to rise out of the dust of despair and achieve unparalleled success? They saw opportunity and had the drive to take advantage of it. They never accepted the notion that their plight was the responsibility of others; they took what they had and made something of it.
>
> "Problems are real. But the 'I am a victim' mentality is far more dangerous than any of the problems we face.
>
> "The New Economy offers a whole new set of challenges and opportunities. Can you embrace the new? Can you rebuild what has been broken, so that you can flourish again in a new era of opportunity?"

The Visionary put his legal pad down and looked out the window at a sea of people heading up and down the street. *There will be winners and losers*, he thought. In that moment, he committed himself to find a few good men and women, people with vision, that would be willing seize these new opportunities. These are the people he would come alongside to support.

"Maybe it's time..."

Prologue

The sun crept slowly above the horizon leaving its shadows on the cluttered floor around the Frustrated Man's desk. He was working his way to the bottom of several piles of papers stacked on his desk before moving to the second tier of priorities arranged on the floor.

Mornings always seemed to be the best time to get things done. It was the one time of the day when there were no interruptions. He loved the quiet. He looked up, it was 6:45 AM and he had already been hard at work for nearly two hours. He paused to take in the song of a bird that landed on the windowsill, the beauty of a magnificent sunrise, and the smell of his third cup of coffee.

The Frustrated Man was the director of a popular nonprofit. In the course of his two decades of service, his organization had touched the lives of thousands. On the shelf behind his desk lay a plaque acknowledging the organization's contributions to the fabric of the growing community of which it had become an integral part.

With these accomplishments came new challenges. The demands placed upon the organization had grown exponentially. As the Frustrated Man and his team struggled to keep up, the economic crisis struck—draining resources, creating deficits, and leaving client needs unmet. The series of spreadsheets on the computer screen in front of him confirmed his fears; every measurable indicator was showing precipitous drops while the need for services was at an all time high.

The carefree bird continued his morning melody. He looked up from the desk and remembered another time.

Ten years ago his organization faced collapse. Created to meet pressing social issues impacting the city, the organization was well received from its beginning. In the first year he received "the rookie of the year award," acknowledging the immediate impact his organization had made in addressing mission initiatives. The organization became the talk of the town.

Positive press and the emotional testimonies of clients fueled demand for services. Financial support, however, was slow in coming. His frustration grew to a point that he was casually referred to as the Frustrated Man. He was ready to call it quits until he met a mentor who guided him to the success that characterized his next ten years.

He smiled. *Those were the days*, he thought. *Some of the most exciting in my life.* He stood from his chair, walking slowly to the window where the bird carelessly sang on. Startled by the movement the bird flew off to a nearby limb.

He glanced at a pile of newspapers on the floor below. The headlines spoke of the crisis that gripped the economy. The stories appearing in professional journals and industry magazines stacked in yet another pile confirmed disturbing losses among nonprofits and universal declines in giving.

Walking back to his desk he looked down at an article he had printed from a blog titled: "Agent of Change or Victim of Circumstance." written by the very mentor who had helped him through the crisis he faced years earlier. The article suggested that nonprofits must change and adapt, or resign to being another statistic; the choice was theirs.

Maybe it's time, he pondered. He walked back to his desk and looked up the phone number of his mentor; the one who had given him hope at his lowest moment. He was simply listed on his contact list as "The Visionary."

"...the current economic crisis is our generation's wake-up call, and in the end it will yield a more productive work force, better organizations, mission realignment, and bring real depth to individuals and organizations."

Chapter One

The New Economy

The Frustrated Man parked his car about three blocks from the office of the Visionary. It was a hot summer day, and a parking spot under a huge oak tree on the edge of a park promised shade. A walk through the park also allowed him to gather his thoughts before the meeting.

Throughout the years he had maintained contact with the Visionary. They would periodically meet at professional gatherings and phone calls were exchanged with some regularity. His mentor always found time for him and was generous in sharing advice on topics of concern.

As he walked past the spewing fountain in the center of the park he reflected on their first visit nearly a decade ago. It was a low point in his career. On one hand, he loved his job. He relished the opportunity to make a difference. The salary wasn't generous, but the intangibles were irresistible. The idea that he could address some of the most troubling issues in the community fueled his passion for his work. The opportunity to impact lives in truly meaningful ways kept him going.

But then the crash occurred—when idealism collided with harsh reality. The initial visit to the office of the Visionary was the last stop prior to submitting the written resignation he left in the envelope on his desk that morning.

Today felt different. If anything had happened over the years that had passed, one thing that seemed to increase was his tenacious spirit. Rooted in the belief that his work was too important to be lost, he needed help in maneuvering through the confusing maze of change. He was frustrated but not without hope.

The sound of traffic signaled that he was drawing close to the park's east gate. Looking up he saw the familiar high-rise building that housed the office of his friend. He passed through the revolving door to the lobby. An open elevator door caused him to jog before the doors closed. Stepping inside he pushed the button labeled 14.

Walking through the glass doors into the open foyer, the Frustrated Man moved to the reception desk. The subtle lighting, earth tone colors, landscape art, "living room furniture," and soothing background music created a comfortable ambiance.

The receptionist looked up and smiled. "So very good to see you again." Her soft smile was genuine and her tone sincere. "He's been asking all morning what time you were coming. Go ahead; just go along in. He's eager to see you."

Returning her smile, the Frustrated Man stepped to the left toward the closed door. Just then the door burst open and the Visionary stepped outside with a huge smile and an outstretched hand. "I thought that might be you," he exclaimed as he warmly shook his hand, "I've been waiting for you all day!" He put his hand on his shoulder and guided him through the open doorway.

"Take a seat. Let me save what I was doing on the computer." He went behind the large mahogany desk, pressed a few buttons, picked up a legal pad and made his way to the leather chair opposite the Frustrated Man.

The office, like the reception area, felt warm and inviting. Indirect lighting, overstuffed chairs, Western art and classic end tables with lamps next to each chair enhanced the intimacy of the setting. More furniture on the other side of the room was available for larger groups.

"Exciting times in which we live, don't you think?" the Visionary asked as he slipped into the seat.

The Frustrated Man smiled. "Exciting? I don't know. Terrifying? Definitely!"

The Visionary returned the smile. "Crisis always precedes change. If everything remained the same we would remain the same. We would stagnate. Nobody wants to do that.

"No," he continued. "This is the wake up call for our generation. Our current economic crisis is a gift for those who can receive it. In the end, it will get leaders on mission, make the work force more productive, and bring real depth to individuals and organizations. These are incredibly exciting days. You'll hardly recognize the world ten years from now. Nothing is being taken for granted in the New Economy."

"The New Economy?" the Frustrated Man asked,

"Yes, the New Economy," responded the Visionary. "This is our generation's Depression. My parents were product of the Depression era. They married in the early '30s and their lives were shaped by the events of their day. I grew up listening to their stories and watching them live. They were thrifty and worked very hard. They saved money and were often critical of my sisters and me for our 'flamboyant' lifestyles.

"They found satisfaction with the little things. Rarely did we take a vacation. When they purchased something, they valued it. They took care of it because they knew the sacrifice they had made to secure it. They were rich in character and learned to live in community. Neighbors and friends helped one another.

"I recently spoke at a large conference of organizational leaders and board members. I asked the crowd, 'How many of you in the last year have had a substantive conversation with a total stranger on the subject of the economy?' I was shocked when virtually everyone in the room raised their hand.

"A shared crisis breaks down barriers. During the Depression, the facades which people erected to distance themselves from others were collectively demolished and what was left was raw and vulnerable. People gravitated to one another in shanty towns called Hoovervilles and found comfort in supporting one another so that together they could gain the strength to survive."

The Visionary seemed lost for a moment in his thoughts. His head leaned back and eyes partially closed as he reached for images of the past in his effort to formulate them into words.

"Yes," he continued, "this is our Depression. It's the most challenging economic environment any of us have ever experienced. And it will change us. Already you can see it. People are saving, keeping things longer, measuring the necessity of every major purchase, working harder, and more appreciative of the small things that were once taken for granted.

"Here's the reality: This isn't going away. The situation is not going to dramatically change. There will be good and bad moments but the impact of what we are going through now will last for years. It will shape the New Economy and either we will learn to adapt to it or we will be the losers. It's make or break time, my friend. Aren't you excited that we're living right in the middle of it?"

The Frustrated Man shifted in his seat before speaking. Measuring words he said, "You're right. We're in the middle of it. But before I can get excited about it, I'm trying to figure out how to survive it."

The Visionary paused, looking deeply into the eyes of his friend with compassion and understanding. Then he spoke. "You and thousands of other individuals like you who manage good and worthy organizations are all in the same boat. There will be catastrophic losses among those who refuse to acknowledge that we're living in the worst economic storm in nearly 80 years.

"But not you, my boy." He slapped his leg, "You are going to be a survivor. I'm here to tell you that the best years of your life and work are still ahead of you. You will come out of this stronger." The tone of his voice was comforting and convincing. The Frustrated Man settled back in his chair as the Visionary continued.

"You will overcome this challenge because you will understand what change has occurred. You will understand how you must look at yourself, present yourself, and redefine yourself. You will make radical changes in some areas. You will see better and more substantive results and you will engage others who will become life-long partners."

The Visionary stopped and the room was silent. Then he concluded, "It's going to be great!"

"There's not a major segment of our society that will not have to make changes in order to thrive in the New Economy."

"...this is reality. This is the New Economy. What you have experienced in the last two years is not going away."

Chapter Two

What in the World Happened?

The two men enjoyed one another. The deep-rooted conviction of the Visionary was expressed passionately. The Frustrated Man drank in his words. Hope, in the New Economy, was hard to find.

A tray of refreshments and steaming mugs of coffee were brought into the room. They sipped coffee, enjoyed a fruit plate, and their conversation continued.

"Now tell me," the Visionary asked, "what changes are you experiencing? What is different now? And how are you dealing with those changes?"

The Frustrated Man had been grappling with the issues these questions raised for the last two years.

His nonprofit was once a perennial favorite of philanthropists in the city, but now it was struggling to stay alive. His major donors seemed paralyzed by fear. His once strong volunteer network was eroding. An overwhelming blanket of apathy seemed to stifle the community as a whole.

The Frustrated Man was slow to respond. He gazed out the window as he sought to formulate a coherent response. "Well," he said, "it's really hard to get a handle on all of this.

"People seem so wrapped up dealing with their own issues they have little time for anything else. Oh, they're kind and act is if they are interested, but their interest doesn't translate into support. I talk and share our mission and vision to address the most troubling issues affecting our community, but it seems like they aren't even hearing me."

The Visionary listened and was clearly waiting for more.

Breathing deeply, the Frustrated Man continued, "Nothing we do is working any more, at least not like it did before. In earlier years, we sent out a letter and we could predict the response. Often the results exceeded our own expectations. A call for volunteers was almost always met with a surge of individuals who made themselves available to do just about anything. In the past, fund-raising events were highly successful, but now we find ourselves hardly breaking even. We've lost hundreds of donors and those who remain are giving about 30% less on average than what they had given in previous years.

"We've cut our budget. That forced us to lay off valuable employees. We've focused on increasing income in every way imaginable, and we still fall behind. I'm beginning to wonder whether it's even worth it. I mean, who really cares? If we were to disappear, would any one notice?"

His exasperation was palpable. The Frustrated Man exchanged glances to the floor, then to the blue sky outside. "I don't know," he mumbled, "and that's why I'm here." He stopped and looked up into the eyes of his caring old friend.

There was a long pause before the Visionary spoke. "Well, they say misery loves company, and you're in good company. You are about the sixth person this month that has come to me and shared a similar story.

"But, for better or worse, this is reality. This is the New Economy. What you have experienced in the last two years is not going away.

"Many nonprofits will experience catastrophic losses. The first to close will be organizations that provide services we like but don't necessarily require. The idea of a private school might have made sense in the old economy but it's perceived as a luxury in the new one. These losses will occur in elementary and secondary private schools. Smaller private colleges will find it increasingly difficult to justify large tuitions that too often require students to incur large amounts of debt in order to finance. Many are beginning to realize that such debt can be debilitating and dangerous at a time when young graduates often marry and are seeking to establish themselves. Expect to see many small colleges making major changes in their efforts to remain viable.

"Smaller nonprofits that have depended on fundraising events to meet annual needs will be part of the first wave of losses.

"Even organizations thought to be safe will be impacted by the New Economy. Everything from churches to entrenched public institutions are feeling the squeeze of less revenue.

"State and local governments, strapped for cash, will look at nonprofits as an untapped source of revenue. Don't be surprised if some or all of your tax exemptions end.

"And government bail outs will soon dry up. Even organizations that receive federal funds must change their ways. There's not a segment of our society that will not have to make changes in order to thrive in the New Economy."

"And that excites you?" the Frustrated Man asked.

"Absolutely," was the immediate response. "Stop and think about it. Almost every meaningful thing that has happened in your life emerged out of difficulty. You were disciplined as a child, and out of that came conviction. You failed a test and developed perseverance. When relationships were challenged, you discovered compromise. Pain and suffering have resulted in some of our greatest medical advancements.

"The same is true today. The New Economy has pulled the rug from underneath an entire population. Could you have imagined that the world would be brought to its knees so quickly by a common crisis? This is unprecedented to the majority of our population, just like the depression of the '30's was to our parents and grandparents.

"And just like that depression produced 'the greatest generation' this one will spawn another who will shape the world of tomorrow."

The Frustrated Man listened as the Visionary spoke. As he listened, a tiny spark of optimism welled up inside. Maybe it would kindle a fire of hope. The Frustrated Man didn't particularly like change, but now he began to welcome it.

"There will be winners and losers," the Visionary continued, "and the big winners will be those who accept the reality that this is the New Economy. They will begin to dismantle entrenched practices in favor of new ways to address the new opportunities that are emerging.

"The changes will be dramatic. I predict that ten years from now we will be talking about how the old days of affluence and indulgence were replaced with more productive and effective methods. A new pragmatism characterized by innovation will yield a sense of community that has been missing in our country for nearly 30 years."

As he spoke, he handed the Frustrated Man a chart.

The New Economy

What's In	What's Out
Frugality	Debt
Simplicity	Extravagance
Function	Theory
Community	Solidarity
Return on Investment	Free Rides
Free Enterprise	Entitlements
Decentralization	Centralization
Challenge Grants	Grants
Small	Large

The Frustrated Man struggled to assimilate these predictions. "It's always easier to go back to what has worked in the past," he said, "embracing change and taking steps into the unknown is ... well, scary."

The Visionary smiled, "Yes, it is. And that's where the winners and losers come in. The winners will step out and lead the way, destroying old paradigms and creating new ones, achieving unparalleled success. The 'late adapters' will spend their time copying the innovators and may survive but not thrive. But the stubborn, who quietly wait for things to come back to where they were, may be lost forever.

"So what will it be for you?"

Stunned by the immediacy of the question, the Frustrated Man took a moment to gather his thoughts. Then he spoke. "What I'm doing is too important to lose. I want to be a winner. I'll take on the challenge, but I'll need help and encouragement along the way. May I impose on you once more?"

"Absolutely!" the Visionary said.

"Your mission, which states why you exist, is the soul of your organization; the degree to which you hold yourself and everyone involved in your organization accountable to guarantee its accomplishment will be at the heart of your success."

"...Constituents and investors in the New Economy will have little time or money to support what they perceive as waste. So in the end you will need to kill your 'sacred cows' or simply let them die of starvation."

"The best way to predict the future is to create it; the best way to build momentum is to develop and communicate a clear vision of how things might be different."

Chapter Three

The Heart of the Matter

The two stood to stretch. This was not going to be a short meeting. They refreshed their coffee cups and the Visionary moved to a small table in the corner of the room. Directing the Frustrated Man to a chair, he sat down opposite him.

"Let's get down to the heart of the matter," the Visionary suggested. "Why does your nonprofit exist? You know the answer because you've spelled it out in your mission statement. Your mission is the soul of your organization. The degree to which you hold yourself and everyone involved accountable to your mission will measure your success."

"Okay," the Frustrated Man said, "but doesn't every organization have a mission?"

"Of course," the Visionary continued, "they had to produce one in order to be incorporated in the first place. Here's the problem: Most mission statements have almost nothing to do with what happens on a day to day basis within an organization."

He continued, "I've found it interesting to ask employees, customers, and vendors to write down the mission statement of an organization. How do they respond? They tell me they don't know what it is. Then I say this, 'That's fine, on the basis of your experience write down what you *think* it is.'"

"I bet you get some interesting answers," the Frustrated Man responded.

"Oh yes," the Visionary smiled, "I went to one large business and presented that assignment to employees. I asked them to write their companies mission statement and told them to submit it anonymously to me."

"What kind of response did you get?" the Frustrated Man asked.

"It was an eye opener for management," the Visionary said. He reached for a paper in the pile on the table next to him, "One employee wrote, *'We exist to make profits so that stockholders can collect dividends and management huge bonuses at the end of the year. In order to accomplish our mission we cut corners, deceive, and manipulate clients and vendors, use inferior materials, and create product life-cycles that enable us to continue to exploit our customer base.'*"

"I bet that opened up a can of worms."

"It did but in the end it was a very healthy exercise. You see, from my perspective we live in a culture that is characterized by individual and corporate narcissism."

"I know what the word means but I'm not sure how it applies to this discussion," the Frustrated Man interrupted.

"It's all about me," the Visionary exclaimed, "individuals have developed this attitude that the world revolves around them. They live their life that way and they end up running their businesses in the same manner. Successful organizations, on the other hand, see the world and their role in it differently. They see clients, communities, and vendors as partners and work hard to do everything possible to engage them in their pursuits.

"Organizations will thrive when they see life

through another set of lenses; through eyes that enable them to imagine how the lives of every human being, community, and country they serve will be touched in meaningful and tangible ways.

"That begins with articulating your vision and then living it out in the things you do."

The Frustrated Man replied, "I'm not sure we talk too much about mission in our organization. We all know what we are here to do and we just go about the job of getting it done."

"That's pretty common," the Visionary said. Then he added, "But if I were to ask you what success for your organization would look like ten, fifteen, or twenty years from now, what would you tell me?"

"That's a big question," the Frustrated Man responded. "It covers a lot of ground. I could tell you what a client would look like, what a volunteer would look like, and what the community would look like. Then it goes a layer deeper. I could tell you what I think they would know and how they would relate to their world."

"Good start," the Visionary replied. "I want you to take the time to write out the specifics of your vision, that is, your idea of success. What does 'mission accomplished' look like for you?

"Years ago I used to ask people about their mission.

It was an important question because every organization has a mission to which they are committed. But over the years I've discovered that mission is often irrelevant."

"What do you mean by that?" the Frustrated Man asked.

The Visionary answered, "Since mission statements are required to incorporate, many organizations made one up in order to meet their obligations, putting little thought into the process. And as time progressed they began developing a unique identity, often far removed from the original mission.

"Oh, there were semblances of the original, but over time they had come to understand what they were good at as an organization and focused on that, sometimes at the expense of other things. Somewhere in the translation the original mission became unclear and ambiguous.

"They also experienced what I call 'mission drift.' Their mission became diluted over time as they moved into new areas that became costly and were not always in harmony with the core mission for which they existed. It's often a subtle change that has a dramatic impact.

"So over the years I've changed my approach. Now I ask a different set of questions like:

"What are you really doing?

"What are you good at?

"What would it look like if you were totally successful in accomplishing your mission?

"I want people to tell me who they really are rather than what they originally thought they wanted to be."

The Frustrated Man nodded. "That makes sense. I can look at all the areas I mentioned: client, volunteer, and community; and come up with a definition of success in each area."

"That's exactly what I want you to do," the Visionary responded. "I want you to carefully examine each component of what you do and then reduce it to a vision statement. Nail down the essence of what you are all about in 30-40 words. Visualize what your real mission would look like in practical terms in 10 years if you were 100% successful in achieving it. That's vision.

"Once we have that, then let's lay it alongside our mission statement and see if the two fit together."

"In other words," the Frustrated Man said, "maybe our mission statement doesn't truly reflect our real mission?"

"Precisely," he responded. "When you know your real mission, you can evaluate your activities. I think you'll find that there are things you're doing that consume time, energy, and finances that are not contributing at all to your mission. Those are the things you need to cut, so you can be free to focus on what you're really all about."

"Gosh," the Frustrated Man said aloud, almost surprising himself, "right off the top of my head I can think of some very expensive endeavors in which we are involved that make little to no contribution to the bottom line of leading us to where we want to go. But many of them are 'sacred cows' that many of our constituents would be very reluctant to let go."

"That's true of your organization and thousands of others. But investors in the New Economy have little time or money to support what they perceive as waste. In the end you will need to kill your 'sacred cows' or simply let them die of starvation."

The Visionary paused to let the last statement sink in before continuing. "I met a college president a number of years ago that shared with me what his college had done to keep mission in the forefront of everything they did."

He reached for another sheet of paper and passed it across the table to the Frustrated Man.

"You can see," he continued, "that at the top of the sheet the mission of the college was clearly stated.

This president understood the mission and was able to articulate it with conviction. One of his annual activities was to bring his senior staff together to review it one-on-one with each of them. At the end of his meeting he would point out the large empty space in the center of the paper. He asked them to return the next week with a quantifiable list of things they planned to do that year that would contribute to the fulfillment of that mission."

"Interesting," the Frustrated Man mused, "he asked them to tell him the things they would do in that year?"

"Yes, and if they didn't get it right the first time, he would send them back until they came up with things that could be measured at the end of the year. If it wasn't quantifiable it would be impossible to measure progress."

"I'll bet that changed the landscape! I can't imagine all your senior staff being that focused," the Frustrated Man responded.

"That's not the half of it," the Visionary continued, "after the president finished with his senior staff he required that they go to everyone who reported to them and repeat the activity. At the end of the process virtually everyone involved in the organization, whether a faculty member, coach, or custodian, was given the same assignment."

"What an incredible way to bring everyone together!"

"Absolutely. In fact it created a new appreciation among staffers of how important they all were in accomplishing the mission. And better yet, once the employee, his supervisor, and the president signed the document it was placed in the employee file and became the basis of the annual employee review that was scheduled in the middle of the year rather than at the end."

"Now that's a great idea," the Frustrated Man stated. "No one wants to be reviewed when it's too late to do anything about whatever negative issues come up. No one wants surprises in their review. No one wants subjective opinions carrying more weight than verifiable, measurable facts. This system eliminates all of that."

"Right you are," the Visionary said, "Employees under this system could measure themselves and find encouragement. It turned out to be a very positive, helpful process for everyone.

"But the bottom line is this: *We must know our real mission and be mission driven.* The real reason an organization exists is to fulfill a mission. There will be many changes in the years to come, but mission is non-negotiable. Method is up for grabs. Methods will change. Old ways are not always the best ways, especially in the era in which we now live. And that's not all bad!"

"...you'll see less business moving overseas as the entrepreneurs of the New Economy will discover ways to perform the same work more cost-effectively here at home. Businesses will become leaner and in doing so more proficient. Cottage industries will flourish, a new independent 'can do' spirit will rise, personal productivity will increase, and people will feel more in control of their destiny."

Chapter Four

The Outsource Rage

A week passed before the next meeting. The Visionary had given an assignment to create a vision statement and the first hour of their next visit was devoted to evaluating that statement and identifying the real mission of the nonprofit directed by the Frustrated Man.

"Mission," the Visionary stated in review, "is the heart of an organization. It needs to be more than a statement; it's a mandate that becomes the basis of evaluating absolutely everything you do. It's the substantive glue that binds together an organization with those who choose to partner with it, the rational component that leads to their meaningful and sustained commitment to you. It must be more than just a combination of words. It's the soul of an organization."

He then transitioned into the next thought. "As you look for ways to stay on mission, expect to outsource more and more, especially in functions that are ancillary to your mission. One of the key characteristics of the New Economy will be the development of new industries spawned by the desire of organizations to preserve resources through outsourcing.

"Let me explain why. As organizations are squeezed by smaller budgets, they find that they must reduce staff or look for people who are willing to work for less than the median wage for a given position. When a staff position is eliminated, part or all of that workload often needs to go somewhere, and outsourcing is the logical alternative. Some firms try to hire staff at cut rate salaries, but outsourcing is smarter."

The Frustrated Man smiled. "In an effort to conserve resources, we hired a bookkeeper two years ago to manage our finances. The board of our organization had a salary range in mind and we pursued candidates based on their willingness to accept our financial offer. We found a candidate all right. But unfortunately we got exactly what we paid for and ended up having to terminate the relationship after learning that our license was about to be revoked for not filing essential documents. What a mess!"

"Exactly," responded the Visionary. "And terminating an employee can be difficult and painful."

The Frustrated Man nodded in agreement, "That's a whole other story that I'd rather not get into right now!"

"I understand," the Visionary responded knowingly. "Unfortunately, many organizations have drifted toward mediocrity by hiring unqualified and inexperienced personnel.

"Organizations can avoid this by focusing on their mission. That's the main thing. In the New Economy outsourcing makes sense for most organizations. How do you save money and get better performance in areas that are ancillary to your mission? You contract with outside agencies. Often their fee will be less than a traditional employee, and they will be infinitely better qualified. The result is better performance at a lower price. Furthermore, if the relationship doesn't meet your expectations you can terminate the contract without creating an internal crisis.

"And outsourcing also makes sense for the individual. As the ranks of unemployed swell, more and more people will want to start taking control of their own destiny instead of passively waiting for an employer to offer them a job. Talented people will figure out how to provide essential services more economically. They will work on a shoestring and in the end will be happier, more productive, more engaged – possibly not as wealthy, but more in control of their own careers. I expect the New Economy to launch a new era of entrepreneurship. This entrepreneurial spirit will rise to meet the vacuum created by the New Economy, and, in the end, everyone will be better off."

"That makes sense," responded the Frustrated Man as he jotted a few notes on the yellow legal pad in front of him. "What other functions do you expect will be outsourced?"

"Everything is up for grabs. Here are some examples: I think you will see accounting moving out of most organizations. Other areas like marketing, public relations, and organizational development or advancement are also likely to be on the list. Since both public and private education is getting hit especially hard in the New Economy, I believe you will see many changes here including a movement to outsource non-academic programs like athletic and arts programs."

"Whew! That's going to get resistance."

"Perhaps, but the costs of managing these programs is strangling the ability of many schools to educate. Elementary and secondary educational programs will eventually be administered much like schools operate in Asia. Schools will provide the core curriculum and everything else will be *a la carte*."

"And offered outside the school?" the Frustrated Man asked.

"Yes. If a child is musical, he will take lessons independently. If she is athletic, she will join a community athletic program. If he is into drama, private troupes in communities will provide opportunities to train and perform.

"But these alternatives must make sense. An athletic facility, for example, run by the Amateur Athletic Union with excellent facilities, training programs for athletes of all ages, professional coaching and training, and competition at a level higher than what exists today could open doors of opportunity for many who would otherwise be lost in the shuffle. The same is true in the arts.

"The door may also be opened to interesting partnerships between groups that formerly ignored one another or competed with one another. For example, there may be partnerships between Christian private schools, home schools and virtual schools.

Colleges will begin looking at strategic alliances as well.

"Even public schools may end up 'out-sourcing' to people already on their payroll to independently manage programs such as athletics and the arts. They may even lease back facilities to those contractors so they have a place to operate but leave it up to them to make it profitable. That will significantly reduce their overhead."

The Frustrated Man was busy jotting down notes as the Visionary spoke. "Is there more?"

"Yes, I think you will see a lot more contract workers in every business, especially nonprofits, You'll see colleges, high schools, and some elementary schools move to hiring more adjunct faculty, often experienced practitioners with a deep understanding of their field.

"In the for-profit sector, I expect to see corporations spin off divisions giving current employees entrepreneurial opportunity to make it on their own. The result? A competitive market . . . quality will improve, value will be discovered, and some of the costly overhead will be eliminated.

"Industry will continue the movement of outsourcing components of their work. I do think you'll see less business moving overseas as the entrepreneurs of the New Economy will discover ways to perform the same work more cost-effectively here at home. In other words, I think there will be a movement to 'solve this problem ourselves' rather than sending it offshore.

"People in our country are resilient. Left alone long enough, need will produce a new generation of entrepreneurs who will lead the way in discovering solutions to many of the troubling issues that have crippled our economy.

"Here are some examples," he added, handing the Frustrated Man a list:

---

10 Areas of Greatest Growth in the New Economy

1. Consulting
2. Technology
3. Online Education
4. Web Development
5. Athletics and the Arts
6. Cottage Industries
7. Alternative Energy Sources
8. Advertising/Branding
9. Computer/Application Programming
10. Online Marketing

"Businesses will become leaner and more proficient. Cottage industries will flourish, a new independent 'can do' spirit will rise, personal productivity will increase, and people will feel more in control on their destiny."

"How should I take this back to my nonprofit?" the Frustrated Man asked.

"Start with this. Look at every position in your organization and honestly ask, 'Does this *really* require a full-time employee?' In some instances the answer will be yes but in other instances you might determine that the work someone is doing could be outsourced. In fact, you might be able to outsource the work to your employee. In other words, your employee will transition out and become an independent contractor or vendor serving multiple organizations."

Now that's interesting, thought the Frustrated Man, *I have a person in mind that I think would love the idea and I think there are things I can do to provide support in what might be a wonderful transition.*

"Things are much different today than they were even five years ago. People generally are afraid; they feel vulnerable. They've never experienced anything like this in their lifetime and learning to adjust to it has been their greatest challenge."

"Share your vision often and purposely show how what you are doing now is strategically taking you down the path to success. Too many organizations lead with their need rather than their vision. But vision motivates people providing you can show evidence that it is more than a pipe dream but a practical possibility."

"People give when they know and are assured in their hearts that it is making a difference."

Chapter Five

Changing Attitudes

After a lunch break, the two men sat down with a steaming coffee latte to continue their conversation.

The Visionary began, "You reported in our first visit that you were seeing changing trends among donors?"

"Yes," responded the Frustrated Man, "giving is

down overall. We have lost many donors outright, and many of our faithful friends have decreased their annual contributions by an average of 20%. That along with reductions in funding we normally receive from charitable foundations, businesses, and other organizations has caused the overall totals for the past year to drop by 38%."

The Frustrated Man paused a moment, looking through the stack of papers in front of him. "Oh, here it is," he exclaimed, "We just completed a capital campaign 18 months ago. People had made pledges to the campaign that they could satisfy over a three-year period. We have been tracking trends pretty closely on this. As of yesterday, payments made against pledges dropped almost 25% over the past year which we're finding somewhat disconcerting given the pledge period is coming to an end."

"That is significant," sighed the Visionary, "but it is pretty much in line of what many industry publications are reporting. Organizations that receive the majority of the gift income from donors who give less than $1,000 per year are the most vulnerable to loss. Larger donors tend to be more rationally committed to the mission and, while they sometimes give less, rarely do they withdraw their support completely.

"The changes you are observing reflect another impact of the economic crisis. The perspectives and priorities of people have changed. Things are much different today than they were even five years ago. People generally are afraid; they feel vulnerable. They've never experienced anything like this in their lifetime and learning to adjust to it has been their greatest challenge.

"Even those with good jobs are concerned that their industry might be hit and that the job they have now might not be there in the future. They're spending less, saving more, and giving an all-out push to eliminate debt exposure should their income decrease through job loss or reduction in salary."

"That's not surprising, I guess," replied the Frustrated Man, "that's what we're doing as well. I just didn't know the rest of the world was taking our lead."

The Visionary laughed. "What influence you have!" Then, more serious, he continued, "Probably, like others, you have decided against making major purchases, postponing or limiting vacations, and are making do with what you have.

"I chatted with a middle-aged couple last week and they told me that they were forced to sell a vacation home. The decision was a traumatic one for them, this home bore evidence of their success and selling it was perceived in their mind as an admission of failure. But as they told me their story they lit up like light bulbs. They shared how they felt released from the financial burden of maintaining two homes, more secure, and a freedom like they hadn't known since early in their marriage."

"That's so interesting," the Frustrated Man interjected, "I've heard stories like that as well. A businessman told me recently that he was forced to lay off more than 40% of his employees. About the time I was beginning to feel his pain he told me that his business was more productive, more profitable, and more alive than ever before. He worked with an outplacement service to help his outgoing staff become productively engaged elsewhere. And he told me that even if things got better, it would be unlikely that he would fill all of the old positions."

"That's it!" the Visionary exclaimed. "People are discovering they can live with less. Frugality can be an adventure, an invitation to experience life rather than being driven by material things. They concluded that they don't need a new car, that the old house is just fine, and finding a bargain at a used clothing store can almost be as fun as buying a new outfit."

"That brings another characteristic of the New Economy. Now, more than ever before, return on investment is key, not just in business, but also in the world of nonprofits." The Visionary reached for an article in a folder next to his left arm. "Here's what I was looking for." Picking up a copy of a newspaper article, "Listen to this headline: 'Nonprofits Beware: Perform or Else!'" He went on, "The article tells us that donors are looking more like investors, still giving, but holding charities accountable for what they do with their gift. They're asking tough questions, requiring accountability, and searching out the best places to give where it's going to make maximum impact."

"It's a new day," the Frustrated Man said.

"Absolutely," the Visionary responded, "There was a time when people gave freely – maybe too freely. They had the money and they gave it away. Now with less money, tough decisions are required. Donors want to wring maximum performance out of every dollar. They want to support agencies where their money will go further. For example, an individual might look at sending $100 to a Romanian missionary as a better investment than to give it to a U.S. college. The $100 will make a real difference in a country where the median income is less than $5,000 per year. Like everything else in life, people are now taking a new look at giving because they want to make certain that their hard earned money is going to make a difference . . . they want to leverage it to the maximum.

"This is why churches with immense debt are losing support. Why would you want to contribute a dollar to pay off a debt when it might better be used in impacting someone's life. Debt ridden organizations will be scaling a big hill trying to convince donors to contribute."

"So, practically speaking, what does that mean for me?" the Frustrated Man asked.

"It means that you need to demonstrate prudence in spending and accuracy in reporting how money was used, how many lives were impacted, and the real difference made through the financial involvement of others.

"People give when they know and are assured in their hearts that it is making a difference. That's why you share stories. Since anecdotes are the most powerful form of communication, tell stories in your newsletters and correspondence sharing the difference that you are making in the lives of those you serve. You will need to convince donors that your organization is worthy of their support. Share your vision often and purposely show how what you are doing now is strategically taking you down the path to success. Too many organizations lead with their need rather than their vision. But vision motivates people providing you can show evidence that it is more than a pipe dream but a practical possibility.

"In the New Economy, you're under scrutiny like never before. And it's because donors no longer want to be spectators, more and more are taking a more active interest in what you are doing and are willing to help you get there.

"Prospective donors are going to require accountability. Serious 'investors' will ask to see financial statements, even audited financial returns. They will want to know what percentage of monies raised really goes for its stated purpose. Organizations like the Salvation Army that boasts that 93% or more goes directly to ministry will continue to be the choice of wiser, more discretionary New Economy philanthropists. Organizations should assume that and be proactive in providing this information before being asked for it.

"Organizations like yours will need to produce annual reports and create a strong 'case' for their worthiness. They must demonstrate in terms that donors can relate to that their use of entrusted funds has been responsible."

> "...what you need more than donors or investors is partners. You need to look at people differently. There's so much expertise and knowledge housed in the minds and hearts of those we know. There are creative people with immense amounts of energy and know how, individuals looking to contribute to something bigger than themselves. If you can learn how to creatively engage people at a different level, recognizing them for who they are and what they have to offer beyond their money, you'll be on the road to success."
>
> "You need to remember that the greatest compliment you can extend to another is to ask them a question."
>
> " . . . in all men's lives at certain periods, and in many men's lives at all periods between infancy and extreme old age, one of the most dominant elements is the desire to be inside the local Ring and the terror of being left outside." – C. S. Lewis, The Inner Ring

Chapter Six

The Need for Partnerships

A week passed before the two men had met. Many of the insights of the Visionary had been rattling around the brain of the Frustrated Man. It was clear that things had changed, that attitudes were different than they had been before. In the New Economy, individuals were not as quick to jump on board the organizational bandwagon.

During the last couple of years the Frustrated Man had begun to notice the glassy-eyed looks he received when explaining his vision to others. They listened. They made eye contact. But it was clear that their mind was a million miles away. Often on his ride home from one of those meetings, he would try to dissect what had happened. In the past, he had been quick to write it off as indifference, but now he understood that this was a product of the New Economy. Consumed by their own needs, people were incapable of grappling with anything outside their own world. What he thought was indifference was really the apprehension created by the uncertainty of the times. Recognizing that provided comfort. It wasn't his mission that led to those glassy-eyed stares. It wasn't his presentation. It was the New Economy.

As he walked into the office of the Visionary that afternoon with a list of questions on his yellow legal pad, he hoped that he could begin to formulate a response to the challenges he faced.

"Good morning!" the Visionary declared to everyone as he burst into the reception area. "Sorry I'm late, there was a horrible traffic tie up on the south side, and I thought I would never get here." Patting the Frustrated Man on the back as the two of them entered his office, he said, "So sorry, chap, to keep you waiting. I hope it's not been too long."

"No, not at all. I have been pondering the things you've shared with me, and I'm trying to figure out what kind of practical response I need to make in the light of what is happening around me."

"Tell me more," the Visionary said.

As they walked to the chairs in the middle of the room, the Frustrated Man began, "Okay. We've lost donors. We've lost volunteers. In the past, we would simply go out and replace them. That's no longer easy to do. In fact, I'm not sure that we can do it. We need to do something different. This is the New Economy. I get that. I understand it. But I'm not sure exactly what to do."

Settling into his seat, the Visionary responded, "I think you're heading in the right direction in the way you're processing this information," the Visionary said. "In the Old Economy when there was a need we quickly looked to individuals who we felt could help us address it by providing the money we needed. And in the nonprofit world we often went to faithful financial supporters and they gave without requiring too much. They trusted us, knew we were doing good work, and had the ability to give generously."

"That's often the way we would approach things," the Frustrated Man nodded in agreement.

"It was the default approach. Have a need; take it to a donor or an investor and hope for the best. And because money was relatively plentiful, they often would respond affirmatively. Then we would go about doing something, without a clear plan. There was a strong trend to almost indiscriminately add employees without clearly knowing the role they would play."

"You're right about that," the Frustrated Man nodded. "One of the first things we were forced to do is to evaluate every position and determine if we could exist without it. It was difficult and pretty sobering."

"Sobering?" the Visionary questioned.

"Yes, sobering in that we came to the realization that we were bloated and that a lot of the resources we had devoted to salaries could have been leveraged more powerfully in the pursuit of our vision. It was also sobering in the sense that our employees needed to make a transition away from employment with us during a challenging economic time. Of course, we helped them wherever we could, but it wasn't easy. Some of our staff had been with us for years. They were like family."

"I hear you," the Visionary said. "I have heard your story repeated over and over again in the last several months. Businessmen tell me that they were forced to lay off scores of employees. But the net result was greater productivity, ownership, and increased community among those left behind. When asked if things were to return the way they were years before, would they hire them back the answer was almost universally 'no.'"

"I guess we get a little sloppy in prosperous times," the Frustrated Man responded with a sense of sadness.

The Visionary continued, "That's true. It is sad to think about the amount of money that has been wasted on sacred cows and programs that did not advance important missions or move good organizations closer to their real vision. We need to change the way we think.

"Now more than ever, in this lean, no-frills, no-waste environment, you need partners. I'm not talking about donors. I'm not talking about investors. I really mean partners. You need to look at people differently. Huge reservoirs of untapped expertise and knowledge are housed in the minds and hearts of those we know. Creative people with immense amounts of energy and know how are looking for a cause bigger than themselves. If you can learn how to creatively engage people at a different level, recognizing them for who they are and what they have to offer beyond their money, you'll be on the road to success."

"That makes sense but how do I do it?"

"Begin at a different starting point," the Visionary said, moving forward in his chair and looking deeply into the eyes of his friend. "I've come to realize that there are groups who are critical to your success. I call them critical groups. A pretty creative name, don't you think?" His eyes sparkled with enthusiasm as he continued.

"Imagine success and then think back and respond to this question, 'If this success were to take place, what groups would have been strategically involved?' Write down all the groups you can imagine."

"You mean groups like business leaders, civic leaders, service club members? Groups like that?" he asked.

"Yes, those groups and probably scores of others like them. But be precise in defining each group. Narrow it down. 'Business leader,' for example is too broad."

"Hang on." The Frustrated Man had taken out his yellow legal pad and was writing feverishly. He looked up and asked, "You mean if I identify businessmen and women I would try to further break down the groups into categories like retailers, manufacturers, wholesalers, service providers, professionals, and any other group I could imagine?"

"Exactly. The more you narrow down a large group, the more effective you can be in meaningfully engaging them.

"Your next step is to prioritize your critical groups. In other words, of all the groups you have listed, which ones could make the greatest impact in terms of helping to move your vision forward?"

"Okay, I can see that," the Frustrated Man said as he continued to write. "What's next?"

"Every critical group has influential members. If I were to give you a directory of the members of the service club to which you belong, could you highlight the names of the most influential members?"

"You mean, in terms of the influence they wield with others?"

"Yes."

"That would take me about 20 seconds," the Frustrated Man replied.

"Exactly," the Visionary nodded, "Every group has influential members. These are the ones that others look to for direction. If you knew all the 'influencers' in all your critical groups, and could seek their input on things of importance to you, would that be valuable to you?"

"Of course it would," replied the Frustrated Man. "But how would I ever get in front of all of these people?"

"Through linkage. You see, you have people within your organization who know many of these individuals. You have friends, volunteers, and donors who might know them as well. The best way to get in front of someone you don't know is to seek the help of someone who does know them to help you."

"But what do I do when I get in front of them? How do I turn them into partners?" the Frustrated Man asked.

"Remember that the greatest compliment you can extend to someone else is to ask that person a question. If you go into the meeting as a learner, you will create the right atmosphere for creating a partnership. Too many people go into these kinds of meetings with an agenda and demonstrate an 'I couldn't care less about how you feel' attitude when talking to the very people who could become valuable partners."

The Visionary paused for a moment. This was such an important point that he didn't want to lose the moment of opportunity to emphasize the simplicity of his method and the profound ways in which it can be effective in engaging partners.

"Of course you share your mission, a bit of your history, and focus on your vision for the future. But remind them that you're not asking for money. You're asking for help. If you fully embrace the concept that people have value that goes way beyond what's in their billfolds, you'll be on the right track.

"Remember, you want to reach the members of a group. But you don't know how. These people of influence do. Seek their help in thinking with you about ways in which you can communicate your message more effectively to those in the group. They know the answers to those questions. You don't. So ask for their input and advice. Let each conversation take its own course, and, at the end, you may walk away with more than you bargained for."

"What do you mean by that?" the Frustrated Man asked.

"In the worst case scenario, those with whom you will be sharing will provide exceptionally valuable and relevant information that you will be able to use. They will respect you; they will know what you do. They will be aware of your vision. You will have strengthened your public image and extended your brand.

"But many times you will accomplish far more than that. If you hear the pronouns change from 'I and me' to 'we and us' something very strategic occurred. Your new friends have chosen to partner with you and that could be invaluable to you in hundreds of different ways."

"Can you give me an example?"

"Sure. I was facilitating a discussion like this one day with a small group. I began asking questions on what might be the best way for me to approach the group of which they are a part. They began by sharing ideas, but, as the conversation continued, they began to offer help. One said that he was a close friend with the Executive Director of a key organization in the city. He picked up his cell phone right then and set up an appointment that afternoon for lunch so that he could introduce me to him. And that was just the beginning! At the end of the meeting this same gentleman scheduled another meeting for this group to get together again next week, giving everyone in the room a list of assignments to fulfill."

There was a long pause. The Frustrated Man wrote down a few things, gazed out the window, and simply thought about what he had heard. After what seemed to be a long period of silence he looked over to the Visionary and said, "This could make all the difference in the world."

"Yes it could," agreed the Visionary. You need partners far more than you need donors and investors. Partners take ownership at a totally different level. They become passionate about what you are passionate about. They engage with you and use their influence with others to move your vision forward. Don't worry about the other things you will require to bring your vision to fruition. That will come!"

"Big is losing its appeal. People like the idea of being in environments where they have a voice."

"People are realizing how they got caught up in self-destructive behaviors that were revealed only through the current crisis. Now people loathe debt and are making aggressive attempts to eliminate it. They are beginning to save again, making more prudent decisions so that they don't ever find themselves in this vulnerable position again."

Chapter Seven

Bigger Isn't Better: Building Community in the New Economy

"People are frustrated," announced the Visionary.

It had been a week since their last meeting and these were the first words out of his mouth as the Frustrated Man walked into his office. A storm was blowing rain against the window behind his desk as the Visionary rose from to greet his friend.

"People are frustrated," he repeated. "That's one of

the primary characteristics of the New Economy. People feel like pawns on a chessboard being unwillingly moved by the will of someone else. And they're exasperated. They are tired of not having a say in their own fate.

"Maybe exasperated is too mild a word," he seemed to be thinking out loud, "No, I think many are just plain angry."

Still stunned by the abruptness of the introduction, the Frustrated Man said, "Wow! What brought this on?"

"I bring this up because it's a key to understanding the New Economy. Most people feel victimized by what has happened. After all, they weren't the ones sitting in high-rise buildings making self-interest decisions that ended up destroying the entire economies of countries around the world contributing to job losses, losses of income, losses of homes, depleted retirement accounts and a host of other troubles that collectively have drained hope from so many. What's left is fear, apprehension, suspicion, ... and anger."

"I'm not sure where you're going with this," the Frustrated Man said as he reached for a legal pad.

"Don't you get it?" the Visionary responded, "People want a say in their lives. None of us want to be herded like cattle. One of the benefits of this crisis is that it has created community. It's the common denominator to which we can all relate because we've all been impacted. As people feel more connected with others they're beginning to discover the benefits of being able to share, empathize, and relate in a much more substantive way than ever before."

"I'm finding that to be true," the Frustrated Man nodded, finally understanding the drift of the discussion. "I was part of a conversation last week with a group of total strangers talking about the various ways we were altering our lives because of the current economic climate"

"Interesting," pondered the Visionary. "Very interesting. I'm curious where did the conversation go?"

"Now that you mention it, it did take some fascinating directions. Some were talking about how their purchasing decisions were impacted. One man, said that prior to this he and his wife were beginning to feel restless and contemplated a move. They have decided to remodel instead, realizing that the money they might lose now couldn't justify a sale. He spoke of eliminating debt, saving more, and reported he was about to make other really tough decisions."

"There you go! This is New Economy thinking!" The Visionary shifted in his chair leaning forward. "When times were good, self destructive behaviors carried fewer consequences. All of that has changed. People are waking up. Now they loathe debt and are making aggressive attempts to eliminate it. They are beginning to save again, making more prudent decisions so that they don't ever find themselves in this vulnerable position again."

"That's exactly what people were telling me," said the Frustrated Man. "In this same conversation, one of the men told me he withdrew his children from a prestigious private school because he could no longer justify $15,000 each year in tuition. Another announced that he had just told his high school senior that she would spend her first two years of college in a community college where she could get her general education courses for a fraction of the cost of the larger private college to which she had set her sights."

He paused for a moment, remembering other conversations that occurred during his meeting. Then he continued, "Another man said he and his family left their mega church to attend a smaller church. When I asked him why he told me that they found a voice there, there was greater opportunity to engage, and that he was tired of just sitting there drinking it in and never having meaningful opportunities to engage at a deeper level."

"Interesting," the Visionary responded. "I'm not sure that those opportunities don't exist in really large congregations but his decision does expose the new ways in which people are adjusting to change. Big is losing its appeal. People like the idea of being in environments where they have a voice. Many who have lost their jobs are beginning their own businesses. Others are joining with colleagues to start new initiatives. They may be operating on a bootstrap, but they find themselves more content than ever before. The have less but they are discovering there are many things that money can't buy."

"Well said," the Frustrated Man responded, "One man told me that once he and his wife got over the shock of the enormous losses they had experienced they rediscovered an aspect of life together they hadn't know since their years of courtship. He reported that now they are talking, saving, and conceiving of ways to do things they normally would have taken for granted."

"Exactly," responded the Visionary. "And it's the same things our parents and grandparents discovered over 70 years ago. They ended up being 'the greatest generation' that contributed so much of what we enjoy today. The same will happen again, just watch! This is our generation's day of opportunity."

"The ones that can first spot the trends and are prepared to answer opportunity will be at the head of the line in the New Economy"

"Insanity is doing the same thing in the same way and expecting different results."

Chapter Eight

Mergers and Strategic Alliances

The two had decided to meet at the local coffee café near the city center. A morning drizzle had slowed the morning rush hour and the Frustrated Man was ten minutes late for their 10:00 AM meeting. He apologized for his late arrival.

"Nonsense," the Visionary responded with his customary gusto. "I always bring a book where ever I go; I welcome delays!"

They chatted over lattes and blueberry muffins. Soon the drizzle subsided and the sun peaked out through breaking clouds. "Let's walk back to the office," suggested the Visionary. "I'll bring you back to your car after our meeting."

Stepping out into the bright sun and warming breeze was a welcomed relief from the morning storm. They took the longer route through the park to the office.

As they walked the Frustrated Man commented, "One of the trends I am noticing are more and more organizations merging in their efforts to remain viable."

"That's an interesting trend," the Visionary said. "Sometimes mergers work but more often than not they are short-term reprieves that fail to address long term issues."

"What do you mean by that?" the Frustrated Man asked.

"Most people think that mergers will result in more income and reduced expenses. In fact, that is realized for the first 12-18 months. But the benefits are short-term. If the business model that created the need to merge isn't addressed, perilous times will reoccur."

"That makes sense," responded the Frustrated Man. "If you continue to build on an unsustainable paradigm that may have created the need to merge, doing the same thing on a larger scale may result in an even greater catastrophe."

The Visionary laughed. "You know the definition

of insanity don't you? Insanity is doing the same thing in the same way and expecting different results. More of the same will not yield different results." The Visionary paused for a moment then added, "If the underlying problems are not addressed, the results will be twice as bad as they would have been!"

"But what about strategic alliances?" asked the Frustrated Man.

"Now that's a different story. This is where I think you are likely to see the greatest changes in the New Economy."

"What do you mean?" the Frustrated Man asked.

He paused, and leaned back, always a sign that there was to be an explanation before there was a response to the question. "Well, in the Old Economy it was an 'every man for himself' environment; everyone looked out for their own interests. And since money was readily available, entrepreneurs and businesses paid often inflated prices for the goods and services they required to get what they needed to fuel their idea."

"Okay," the Frustrated Man said, somewhat confused, "is there something wrong with that?"

"Every idea, every business proposition requires others to facilitate. But now, with a tighter lid on borrowing, there's less working capital to fund new initiatives yet there is a surplus of well qualified and capable people."

"I'm beginning to see an idea unravel," the Frustrated Man said, smiling.

"Good!" the Visionary exclaimed. "New Economy thinking approaches challenges with a different, more cooperative outlook. Winners in the New Economy are going to others with a different approach. There will be more bartering occurring among individuals and companies. Rather than engaging professional services for a price, they might seek the help of others by offering them a percentage of the business they are seeking to build or a portion of profits yet to be realized."

"Interesting," the Frustrated Man pondered. "My guess is that they will take a greater interest, probably do a better job, and maybe even suggest better options to maximize the productivity of the initial idea."

"Right you are," the Visionary said, slamming his fist on his leg. "That's New Economy thinking! When people have an ownership in something they give greater care to its well-being. At the end of the day you get a better product, more engaged involvement, and a new sense of community as people come together. This change in the way we do business will allow individuals to take charge of their lives rather than seeing themselves as victims or as meaningless pawns in a grand game. Remember, everyone has something to offer. The real geniuses in the New Economy will be the ones who find ways to connect people through strategic alliances."

"Can you give me other examples?" the Frustrated Man asked.

"Sure," the Visionary responded, "consider education. Many are raising legitimate questions about what is really essential to the mission of preparing students to take their place in our changing world. Things that have become part of education, like athletic and arts programs, will be under scrutiny. I believe you will see a growing trend to out-source these to the private sector.

"Just in the area of athletics, I am working with several organizations who are building facilities to accommodate the growing need of communities to provide these services. These groups believe so strongly that this will be the case that they are developing strategic alliances with suppliers, builders, coaches, and others who can shape the future of community-based athletics.

"They believe that outsourcing is the answer and that the private companies will be able to produce better training facilities, better coaching, and better competition than what is currently available. They could be professionally run and managed for male and female athletes of all ages. And the organizations that have joined together recognize that they can deliver facilities and programs that are both affordable and profitable.

"For them, athletics will be their mission. They will focus on delivering the best possible programs enabling schools to stay focused on their core mission, educating students."

"So," the Frustrated Man said, "if I'm understanding you correctly, you are saying that even in the New Economy there will be growth and development."

"Oh yes," the Visionary responded. "In fact that's where the winners will flourish. The ones who can first spot the trends and prepare to answer opportunity will be at the head of the line in the New Economy.

"Of course, we're just talking about athletics now. The same will be true in the arts and a variety of other areas. Imagine young musicians and artists enjoying a place where they can be trained and nurtured in their skills by individuals committed to getting the very best they have out of them."

"So these things are being offered *a la carte*, right?"

the Frustrated Man asked.

"Yes," the Visionary responded. "This is how it's done in other parts of the world with great success. It's foolish to think one organization can offer everything and do it with excellence. We need to focus on what we do best and do it better than anyone else."

"Is that a New Economy thing?"

The Visionary smiled. "Now you're beginning to get it. New Economists will demand it. They're tired of mediocrity and they're demanding value in everything. They're looking for return on investment and as long as private enterprise controls it, they can shop to get what they want."

"Everybody wins?"

"Everybody!"

"You see the problem with most organizations is that they are married to both their mission and their method. We ought to be married to our mission. That's why we exist. But method is another thing. Organizations that are married to the same old way they've always done things are going to be the losers in the New Economy..."

"But the point remains. Don't ever forget that while changes are occurring, the mortar that will make them work is the same that you used ten years ago. Don't forget the rules, use them diligently and the end result will be even greater success. You've built a solid infrastructure; use it to build again in the New Economy."

Chapter Nine

Some Things Never Change

As they continued their discussion back at the Visionary's office, the noon hour came and went. Their conversation was interrupted by the loud blare of a weather siren.

"Oh," the Visionary said, somewhat startled, "It must be 1:30. It goes off every Tuesday at 1:30!" He jumped from his chair and smiled, "I wondered why my stomach was beginning to growl. I'm really hungry."

"You know, I just discovered this little bistro down the street. They've got a pastrami sandwich that is delectable. Let's run over there and continue our discussion."

The bistro was a bustle of activity. The lunch crowd was just leaving and tables were becoming vacant. It was apparent that this was a popular place as groups throughout the restaurant engaged in meaningful discussion while munching on their food.

"Perfect," the Visionary blurted out, "couldn't have done better if I planned it!" The host escorted them to the requested table in the corner.

"Don't even bother to look at the menu," he said, "you want the Pastrami Reuben. You like pastrami, right?"

The Frustrated Man nodded, quickly realizing that his choice had already been made.

"Wonderful," he said. A young waitress approached the table with menus. "Oh, don't bother with that, dear," he said, "just bring us two Pastrami Reuben sandwiches, two cups of the Roasted

Tomato soup, and some bread. Water would be fine, we'll have two skimmed lattes for dessert."

Like everything he did, the Visionary wanted to get past the details so he could continue developing thoughts that seemed always to be rumbling through his mind.

"Look around you," he said. "Here is a business that is thriving in the New Economy. How do they do it? They have worked hard to create a comfortable environment, a place where people feel welcomed, almost like family." He picked up a tent card on the table and showed it to his friend, "Look at this," he continued, reading its message, "'Join us for breakfast, stay for lunch!' What a powerful message! It communicates that we're more concerned about your experience than simply turning a table so we can make more profit. It's paying off for them."

The Frustrated Man looked around the bistro, noticing little groups still deeply engaged in conversation, while others sat with laptops and lattes. The staff was friendly, but not intrusive. It really did feel comfortable, almost like home.

The Visionary interrupted his thoughts. "Remember ten years ago?" he asked.

"You mean when I came to your office about ready to join the Peace Corps?"

The Visionary nodded.

"How could I forget?" the Frustrated Man said. "You rescued me, giving me the tools I needed to build my organization on a solid foundation. You taught me how to build the relationships that made our nonprofit successful. Your involvement in my life is the reason I have achieved. More importantly, thousands of lives have been changed as a result of what you did for me."

"Nonsense," the Visionary answered. "You're the reason things changed. I just gave you some tools. You took them and built one of the most successful and respected nonprofits in this city."

He continued, "That's what I want to talk to you about. We live in a time of change. Organizations are taking a new look at themselves, a much more critical look than ever before. From the outside it seems like chaos but I'm totally convinced that the changes driven by the New Economy are going to change the face of the world as we have known it. And that's exciting to me. Very exciting.

"Those who are on the cutting edge will thrive. That's where you need to be. You must imagine and implement creative ways to achieve your core mission. You must move quickly and act decisively lest you lose some of the incredible opportunities before you.

"Part of that process will be uncomfortable. But in the midst of the organizational revival that will take place you need to remember that some things never change."

"Like what?" the Frustrated Man asked.

"Like relationships," the Visionary answered without a moment of hesitation. "At the end of the day, just like ten years ago, an organization's effectiveness will be measured in terms of how effective they have been in building relationships.

"In addition, the rules of development are still in place, alive and well. The time honored principles of cultivation, bridging, and planning are all the same. These things you can count on. This is the mortar that holds the building blocks together. You can't forget that."[3]

The waitress interrupted the conversation for a moment as she brought the biggest sandwich the Frustrated Man had ever seen. The pastrami must have been six inches high in the middle. A combination of melting cheese and Thousand Island sauce oozed from the middle of the sandwich, dripping on the napkin below.

"*Bon Appetit!*" she said, dismissing herself so they could continue their talk.

---
[3] For a detailed treatment of these principles, see *Funding Your Vision: New Hope for Non-profits* (2000) by Gerald Twombly.

"Now," the Visionary said, looking at the feast before them, "taste this soup before you try the sandwich. The dollop of sour cream makes it! Mix it in slowly and carefully, you'll love it. Nothing like it!"

They sipped the steaming soup and the Frustrated Man spoke. "I appreciate the reminder. But, to be honest, I still struggle a bit with change."

"Understandably," the Visionary replied hardly looking up from the soup he seemed to be enjoying thoroughly. "You see the problem with most organizations is that they are married to both their mission and their method.

"We ought to be married to our mission. That's why we exist. But method is a another thing. Organizations that are married to the same old way they've always done things are going to be the losers in the New Economy.

"You know, I think the world we'll see ten years from now is going to look a whole lot different than what we see today," his eyes gleamed, almost sparkled with excitement. "You might not even recognize a church and education is going to be totally revolutionized. Delivery systems will change, efficiencies will dramatically improve, you'll see leaner operations, and more of them. It's going to be wonderful."

"Easy for you to say," the Frustrated Man smiled.

The Visionary returned his smile. "Even though I'm not on the front lines like you are, I'm still in the fight. But the point remains: While changes are occurring, the mortar that will make them work is the same that you used ten years ago. Don't forget the rules. Use them diligently and the end result will be even greater success. You've built a solid infrastructure; use it to build again in the New Economy."

> "...every business is organized perfectly to accomplish what it is it is currently accomplishing; if what you are accomplishing isn't taking you where you want to go then change is essential."

Chapter Ten

The Turning Point

The Frustrated Man leaned back in his chair. The sun crept up over the eastern hills as he watched the beginning of a new day.

His sleep that night had been restless. So much of what he had gleaned the past several weeks from the Visionary made sense. And while he realized that things had changed, perhaps forever, he still found himself longing for days gone by. It was easier then. He built a circle of faithful donors, shared an opportunity, and needs were met. But now things were different; that was inarguable. And the changes shook his world.

Decision time. The thought made him uneasy. It was time to make hard decisions, decisions that would change his future, and change the future of many other people – staff, board, volunteers, donors and clients of the organization he represented. The right choice ... or the wrong choice ... in either case, the consequences would not be small. His decision would take many people into a new place.

Several conversations had occurred during this time with members of his board. They agreed with him; the world is changing. "We need to change to survive," the board president agreed. But what changes? The board asked him for a list of recommendations. It was that request that kept him awake throughout the night, pondering possibilities and weighing their potential impact.

Change. The very idea of it made him restless. Just at the time when he began to feel comfortable, the economic crisis hit. It couldn't have come at a worse time. Only months before the organization had announced the expansion of programs and services and overnight, at least it seemed, the ability to fund them disappeared.

He thought back at his early conversations with the Visionary.

He had been reminded that crisis is the mother of innovation; that many of the great accomplishments of mankind were often birthed in the most difficult of times. Now was his time, and he knew that. But fear of failure still stalked him.

In his lap was the legal pad he had used to take

notes during his visits with the Visionary. He looked through them carefully, taking a yellow highlight pen noting points of particular relevance to his situation.

Mission never changes, but methods are up for grabs. He pondered that thought. He circled a quote that had been given to him by the Visionary in one of their earlier conversations:

> "*The future belongs to a very different kind of person with a very different kind of mind—creators and empathizers, pattern recognizers, and meaning makers. These people—artists, inventors, designers, storytellers, caregivers, consolers, and big picture thinkers—will now reap society's richest rewards and share it's greatest joys.*"[4]

I want to be that kind of man, he thought. The Visionary had continually emphasized the point that there would be winners and losers in the New Economy, and he was determined to come out on top. He circled another note.

> *Every business is organized perfectly to accomplish what it is it is currently accomplishing; if what you are accomplishing isn't taking you where you want to go then change is essential.*

And another:

---

[4] *A Whole New Mind,* by Daniel H. Pink, page 1.

> "...the capabilities we once disdained or thought frivolous—the 'right brain' qualities of inventiveness, empathy, joyfulness, and meaning—increasingly will determine who flourishes and flounders."[5]

He set the legal pad down and looked heavenward. "How do I do this?" he whispered.

He looked back out the window, and a memory came to mind. He was in a church class in when he was about thirteen years old. The teacher, one of his favorites, was telling the story of Moses, being chased by a pursuing army, standing on the shores of the Red Sea with no place to go. An entire nation was looking to Moses for direction, bitterly complaining of the disaster that seemed imminent. The Lord appeared to Moses that day and said:

> "Why are you crying out to me? Tell the nation...to get moving. Hold your staff high and stretch your hand over the sea. Split the sea! The Israelites will walk through on dry ground."[6]

The Frustrated Man smiled as he remembered his teacher's words: "Sometimes God brings you into situations over which you have no control and into places where there is no place to turn. It's then you have to put your trust in Him and move forward.

---

[5] Ibid. page 3.
[6] Exodus 14:15, *The Message*

You will come to that point many times. Take what you know and, armed with faith, move forward into seas of uncertainty. You will find the strength you need and have the incredible experience of seeing God at work."

I'm in one of those moments, the Frustrated Man thought to himself. *This is the biggest challenge I've faced so far. I've been on cruise control long enough. I must make a decision. Do I retreat and hope for the best? Or do I step forward and trust God for the results?*

The image of the Red Sea parting and the Israelites walking across on dry ground filled his mind. The Frustrated Man smiled.

"I will be a New Economy thinker," he said out loud. "I will not sit here and watch this work of a lifetime dwindle away. I will step forward and do what I know I need to do."

A feeling of determination gripped him. *Change always involves risk,* he thought. *Living out in the fringe may not be comfortable, but the choice is clear. I will do what I must and put my confidence in God.*

"We have to reject the notion that someone owes us something. The entitlement society has lost the free enterprise spirit that made our country great. We're all too quick to blame someone else and hold out our hands for help. If throwing money at problems were the solution to the problems plaguing society we would have no problems."

Chapter Eleven

New Economy Thinking

There was a spring in his step as the Frustrated Man walked into the office of the Visionary on this bright morning.

"You look chipper," the Visionary said, looking up from a pile of papers on his desk.

"I feel like I'm in a much better place inside. I've had a chance to work through some things. I'm ready to start making changes. I've faced my fears. For me, that's a big step forward."

The Visionary nodded as he picked up the cup on his desk and make his way to the comfortable chairs in the center of the room. "Fear keeps us from change. While most of us can embrace the need for change intellectually, making decisions that have consequences is a whole lot harder."

"I am afraid," the Frustrated Man replied. "I'm not sure I would share that with many people. But there's a lot at stake here. It's not always pleasant being the leader to whom others are looking for direction. Sometimes I would just like to fade away in the background and let somebody else take the shots."

"I understand," the Visionary replied with sincerity in his voice. "You know, I was reading about a conversation that took place in 1985 between Andy Grove the co-founder and former CEO of Intel with its current leader, Gordon Moore." As he spoke, the Visionary reaching through his files for the article he wanted. After a sigh he found it and began:

> "Grove asked Moore a question: 'If we got kicked out and the board brought in a new CEO, what do you think he would do?' Gordon answered without hesitation, 'He would get us out of memory.' Grove stared at him, numb, and then said, 'Why shouldn't you and I walk out the door, come back and do it ourselves.'"[7]

"What an incredible, dispassionate way to examine our response to the New Economy," the Visionary

---

[7] *What the Best CEOs Know.* by Jeffrey A, Krames, 2003, pg. 138.

said. "Forget the old paradigms and forge ahead with the new."

"You know," he continued, "I think you know the answers. I think you know what you should do, but you allow yourself to be trapped by where you are."

"Wow," the Frustrated Man cringed, "You may be right. But your quote is helpful. What would a new leader do if he or she took my place? That makes it easier to think through what my real priorities are."

"I think so," the Visionary nodded. "Do you know what you would do?"

"I think so," the Frustrated Man responded. "We exist to help people but what we end up doing mostly is giving them what they perceive they need. If I were to come back I would set up micro-businesses for our clients, giving them the opportunities to use their gifts and skills to help themselves."

His face brightened and he begin to speak more rapidly, his arms motioning as if that might help to make sure his words were being heard.

"Think about it," he continued looking at the Visionary squarely in the eyes, "these would provide life experience, provide income to the workers, and generate profits. That would reduce our overhead and, consequently, our financial dependence on donors."

"Now you're thinking!" the Visionary said, finding it difficult to stay seated. "That's New Economy thinking. We have to reject the notion that someone owes us something. The entitlement society has lost the free enterprise spirit that made our country great. We're all too quick to blame someone else and hold out our hands for help. If throwing money at problems were the solution to the problems plaguing society we would have no problems."

"Well, I didn't mean to get you so excited," the Frustrated Man responded, laughing aloud.

The Visionary smiled. "You know, I find so many people so busy bemoaning their situation that they are blinded to the opportunities in front of them." As he spoke, he shuffled through some of the papers in front of him.

"Look," he continued, here's another Andy Grove quote I love:

> *"Most companies don't die because they are wrong; most die because they don't commit themselves. They fritter away their momentum and their valuable resources while attempting to make a decision. The greater danger is in standing*

still."[8]

"I think that's the conclusion I came to this morning," the Frustrated Man responded. "I knew some of the things we needed to do but I just couldn't bring myself to making a decision that was going to be initially unpopular. I feel like I have the strength to do it now.

"In fact, I'm ready to do what Andy Grove suggested. I'm ready to walk out of the room, dump the old paradigms, and walk back in ready to make changes. I'm ready to be my own successor."

"So it begins," said the Visionary with a smile.

---

[8] Ibid, page 131.

"Vision is at the heart of capturing the imaginations of others. We're all emotional creatures and we are first moved by emotion before rationalism creeps in."

"A lot of people die with their vision."

"It is vision...that captures the imagination and motivates us to move forward."

Chapter Twelve
Strategic Planning

Things were beginning to come together in the mind of the Frustrated Man. The Visionary's admonition to imagine what his successor might do on his first day on the job if he were relieved of his responsibilities was a catalyst to act upon what he already knew needed to be done.

In preparing for their next meeting, he began to write down the questions for his mentor. While the direction seemed clear in his mind, execution was still cloudy.

The front page of his legal pad included circles, lines, and scattered thoughts expressed in pithy statements in the margins. He looked at his watch as he examined the sheet. He was to meet with the Visionary in just half an hour.

In his hurry to make the morning's meeting, he grabbed everything on his desk, threw it into a back pack, and left his office on the run announcing to his assistant he would be back before lunch.

He arrived a few minutes before their scheduled appointment. Gathering his thoughts, the Frustrated Man took a deep breath and walked into the office of his mentor. After exchanging greetings and getting personal updates, the Frustrated Man moved directly into his agenda. "I've been doing a lot of thinking," he began, "and I've settled in on some ideas that I feel we need to consider if we're to move forward in our organization.

"I have ideas, but I don't have a plan." He went on to sketch out some of his thoughts.

The Visionary listened intently and then began, "Great stuff. Really. You have conceptualized your mission and are beginning to recognize the steps you need to take in order to get from where you are to where you want to be.

"Where you want to be is your vision. Vision equals mission accomplished. And vision will capture the imaginations of others. We're all emotional creatures and we are first moved by emotion then by logic."

The Frustrated Man smiled. "That's interesting that you would say that. As I was driving over here today I saw an incredibly beautiful car. I had never seen something quite like it and I quickly picked up my speed to see exactly what kind of car it was."

"An expensive one, I imagine," the Visionary chimed in.

"Yes. For a minute I thought this is the kind of car I would like to own; I mean it was incredible. But then I began to laugh out loud; I couldn't afford the gas to fill it up to say nothing about the price of the car. It was pretty emotionally appealing but then hard reality set in!"

"Good point," the Visionary responded. "But emotion is still important. You were first attracted to your wife for emotional reasons. We were attracted to a church, service club, and even the home you live in for the same reason. There comes a time, however, when you are left to process. You investigate pros and cons, you assess longer-term issues like maintenance and sustainability. At the end, you make your decision based on reason.

"But it is vision, a clear conceptualization of what *could be* that captures the imagination and motivates us to move forward. Take marriage, for example. Saying vows and committing yourself to one another for the rest of your life doesn't guarantee a successful marriage any more than joining a church, service club, or even buying a home guarantees that you will experience what it means to be engaged and fulfilled.

"One of the exercises I like to walk people through is to imagine success. If your marriage, for example, were everything you imagined it might be 20, 30, or 40 years from now, what would it look like? What would the children born into that relationship look like? What would they know? How would they relate to others? How would they relate to the world in which they are a part?

"That's vision," he exclaimed as his obvious enthusiasm for the topic rose. "Without it you lose interest. When organizations like yours fail to keep the larger vision in front of friends and constituents eventually you will see a dwindling of enthusiasm and interest. People want to go somewhere and be led by someone who has a road map to get there."

"I want you to live in the future; to imagine you have already succeeded. Once you do that you will need to assess where you are and what needs to occur in order to move you toward your goals."

"Ah," the Frustrated Man breathed aloud. "This is exactly where I wanted to go today. I can think conceptually but I'm not good at creating a road map."

"That's the case with most of us," the Visionary agreed. "Many people die with their vision. They want to make a difference, they have the capability of leading an organization to achieve it, but nothing ever happens. Do you know why?"

"Because they don't know how to do it?"

"Exactly. They have never taken the time to identify the steps that will take them from where they are to where they want to go."

The Visionary continued, "Some of the most intriguing people I have come to know over the last several decades lived in another world. They were visionaries and everyone around them became captivated by the vision that consumed them. They took the time to articulate their vision in a variety of different ways, shared it incessantly with everyone around them, and convinced all of them, or at least a great majority, that a plan was in place that would get them there.

"Incredibly, however, only 12% of organizations have a strategic plan. The defining characteristic of a strategic plan is that it is quantifiable. In other words, you quantify all the things that need to be done and begin to schedule them over a period of time. It might take weeks, months or years to implement a strategic plan, but the plan is always quantifiable. When a step is completed you cross it off. *Plans that lack quantification aren't plans at all, they're just good ideas."*

The Frustrated Man shook his head. Over the years, he had hundreds of good ideas most of which never saw the light of day.

"So why don't leaders plan?" he asked. "If only 12% of organizations have a strategic plan in place, that means 88% don't!"

"Yes, that's right," the Visionary responded. "There are any number of reasons why. Most organizations have attempted planning but too often nothing comes out of it. What they thought was a good idea ended up discouraging more people than encouraging them. Nothing ever happened and people finally lose hope and go away."

"But why don't things come together?"

"Because you can't divorce an idea from what it will require to bring it to reality. You can't plan without counting the cost, literally. What are you prepared to invest in money, time and other resources? Plans also fail because they are created by people with an agenda instead of a balanced team whose members can bring diverse perspectives to the table. Plans must be created by the right people who know exactly what can be committed to a given initiative. Plans are useless if the right people are not available to give the project the kind of sustained support it needs to succeed. Plans that have been created within a vacuum, especially a financial one, are often irrelevant and are rarely implemented."

"I see that a lot in my world," the Frustrated Man agreed. "Because of it, people who were once excited about an organization lose interest and disappear."

"Too often that's the case," the Visionary acknowledged. "Plans must be built within the context of practical realities. That doesn't mean they have to be limited in terms of size, the limits are driven by their realistic potential to mobilize resources at the time they are needed."

"Okay, how do I plan?" the Frustrated Man asked.

"Step one: Begin with your vision," the Visionary said. "What would every aspect that you are planning look like if you were 100% successful in achieving your mission?

"Step two: assessment. Lay your vision alongside reality and give yourself a grade. Think of it in terms of letter grades, A, B, C, or D. Where are you? If your current reality looks like your vision, then you get an A. If it is totally removed from your vision, then you get a D."

"Well I doubt it would be an A," the Frustrated

Man said. "If it were perfect now I wouldn't have a vision for it!"

"Exactly," the Visionary agreed. "Now comes step three: Once you've given yourself a grade, ask yourself why you assigned the letter you did. In other words, if you gave yourself a C, why?"

"I'm guessing there would be many reasons."

"You're right. List them all."

"Okay, then what?"

"Step four: Prioritize the deficiencies you identified in an order that reflects the priority in which you feel they should be addressed."

The Frustrated Man's eyes brightened. "Ah, it's beginning to come together."

The Visionary smiled. "I hope so. You can't plan anything until you've done these initial four steps.

"Step five is where planning begins. Often you will need to blend priorities because working on one priority has profound implications for another. The blended list then needs to be scheduled over a period of time based on your ability to resource each initiative with the dollars, time, and people required to get it done. Plans often address many issues, each of which will require your attention. You can't implement initiatives to address all of your issues all at once because you have limited resources and limited time. So you create a plan that helps you get it done over a reasonable amount of time. Then you organize yourself, and begin taking people with you on the journey to your vision.

"Step six requires putting in place an organizational infrastructure to support achieving the plan. From there you implement the plan taking time each year to evaluate progress."

"This is great," the Frustrated Man breathed. He glanced down at the notes on his legal pad:

| Step 1: Picture the ideal. |
| Step 2: Assess reality. Give yourself a grade. |
| Step 3: Find out why. |
| Step 4: Prioritize. |
| Step 5: Create a Plan. |
| Step 6: Organize. |
| Step 7: Implement. |
| Step 8: Evaluate. |

"As simple as that," the Frustrated Man asked.

"As simple as that!"[9]

---

[9] Jerry Twombly has written a book outlining the details of this process entitled *An Organizational Planning Primer*. It is available on Jerry's blog: www.jerrytwombly.com.

"The idea of branding is to capsulize the perceptions you would want individuals to have concerning your organization."

"Marketing represents the efforts an organization makes to reach a large audience with a message that will help the company gain awareness among consumers and a level of credibility."

"...marketing stops once you walk in and that's when, in this case, sales begin. Once you move from communicating to market segments and start looking at customers as individuals the sales process begins."

"...marketing may get you to the door but it won't make the sale!"

Chapter Thirteen

Marketing, Sales and Rebrands

The Frustrated Man began the long process of planning suggested by the Visionary. He was tired of good ideas that never saw the light of day. As he worked, he felt empowered. The plans would enable his organization to make a difference. His team could change their world.

He knew that the New Economy would demand change and that his organization must prepared to act in these historic and unparalleled days of opportunity.

As he planned for his weekly appointment with the Visionary, he began to compile a list of questions for his mentor. The questions revolved around a central theme: "How can we market our new vision to our constituencies?"

The Frustrated Man drove through the garden parkway leading to the restaurant where their meeting was scheduled. As he did, he marveled at the beauty of the day. With temperatures in the low 70's and low humidity, it was perfection. High cirrus clouds dotted the deep blue sky like broad feathers and birds chirped in a chorus of celebration.

The magnificence of the day had not been lost to the Visionary. He had called earlier that morning suggesting that they meet at the Patio Restaurant alongside a small lake on the edge of town. He had reserved a secluded tree shaded table close to the lake.

"What a marvelous day!" the Visionary said as his friend was escorted to the table. "So good to see you. I could hardly imagine being inside on a day like today."

The next ten minutes were spent in catching up. Each had laid papers on the table, was sipping sweet tea, as the Frustrated Man began, "I've spent the last week working on the preliminaries of what I believe is a new and improved plan that will enable us to be even more effective in accomplishing our mission. But since it's such a departure from what we have been, it seems that there's a great deal we need to do to present our new vision to those we seek to serve."

Shuffling his seat in order to have a more direct look at his friend, the Visionary responded, "You're right. You need to rebrand your organization, market that new brand message strategically and aggressively, and begin the sales process. That's the challenge the lies before you."

Reaching for a pen, the Frustrated Man grabbed his forever-present legal pad and quickly jotted down three words. He looked up and said, "You mentioned three things: branding, marketing, and sales. What is the difference?"

"Let's start with the perceptions people have of you. People have perceptions of your organization that have been gained through a variety of sources. You have been 'branded' almost by default. The idea of branding is to capsulize the perceptions you would want individuals to have concerning your organization. Sometimes it's reflected in an attractively designed logo that carries with it a message that communicates something non-verbally to those familiar with it."

"For example?" the Frustrated Man asked.

"Well take an Apple. What do you think about when you see the an Apple on a bill board?"

"I think of computers, phones, and other innovative products produced by a first-class company," he quickly responded.

"But all you saw was an Apple. Years ago, you might have thought about applesauce or apple pie. But now you saw a very distinctively designed logo that communicated computers, iPods, iPhones and other technology to you. The company produced the logo but their marketing and sales efforts defined that logo in such a way that you have drawn the conclusions you stated. My guess is that anyone from Apple Computer would have been pleased by your answer," the Visionary said, smiling.

"You have similar responses to the Nike Swoosh, the McDonald's arches, or the Starbucks Coffee sign on a highway billboard. People begin to relate messages from a simple visual picture, in this instance a logo.

"But sometimes things change and that requires the need to rebrand yourself. That will take effort and energy at every level within your organization. Your brand could be communicated by your logo; it could be supported by a typeface, or a series of complementary images all designed to create perceptions without the need of verbal explanation."

"I think that makes sense. Recently I noticed that McDonald's began a new emphasis upon coffee," the Frustrated Man stated, "and it seems they are now beginning to market themselves differently."

"A very good point. A brand communicates a message but is not sufficient in itself to market your organization. For years when you saw the Golden Arches, you immediately thought of Big Macs. But McDonalds realized that it was essential for them to adapt their business model to accommodate changes in the culture.

"Their coffee was never particularly good," the Visionary continued with a broad smile, "at least I never thought so! So it became essential that they create a new vision in the minds of the coffee consumer. The new McDonald Café logo along with a broad selection of menu items distinctively prepared and competitively price needed to be incorporated in their brand message."

"Okay, that makes sense. But what about the organization whose performance doesn't match their message?" the Frustrated Man asked.

"A great point," the Visionary exclaimed, "That can be disastrous. That's where marketing and sales come in."

"Marketing and sales – what's the difference?"

"Marketing represents the efforts an organization makes to reach a large audience with a message that will help the company gain awareness among consumers and a level of credibility. You will see marketing occur in television commercials, you'll hear it on the radio, and read about it in magazines, newspapers, and billboards. I was driving down the highway last week and saw a billboard with a cheeseburger. It looked so good that I pulled off at the next exit to stop and get lunch."

"Well, it worked, right?" the Frustrated Man asked thinking this was all a bit too simple.

"To a point," the Visionary agreed, "but suppose I had walked in and the restaurant was dirty, the lines extraordinary long, and the restrooms filthy. In that case, I might have changed my mind. Marketing stops once you walk in and that's when, in this case, sales begin. Once you move from communicating to market segments and start engaging with customers, the relationship process begins.

"A friend of mine came up with an interesting graphic that creatively puts all of this together[10].

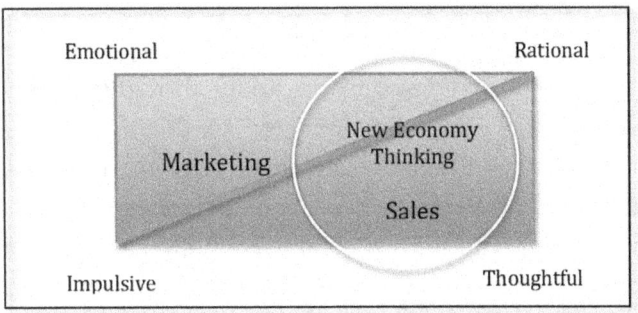

"There are some decisions that we make that are impulsive, decisions that are driven more my our emotions than through thoughtful analysis. That would include things like cheeseburgers, an iPhone application, a newspaper you might purchase from a sales rack next to the check-out line at the grocery store. But there are other decisions that require a good deal of thought, things like purchasing a house, a car, or committing yourself to $25,000 annual tuition payment for a college bound son or daughter.

"In the first example the marketing drove the sale. It was the picture of the cheeseburger that took me off the highway into the restaurant, the attractive

---

[10]   This chart appears in the unpublished manuscript titled: *360 Degree Sales Logic* by Chad M. Twombly.

advertising for the 'all-in-one' application that would forever eliminate the need for another, or the 'must read' article in the paper prominently displayed in the check-out line.

"But when it comes to the more thoughtful decisions, marketing may get you to the door but it won't make the sale. The sales price of the house must match up with need and capability, the same would be true with the car, or whether or not you choose one college over another. It's the sales process, *a relational encounter*, that will determine whether people buy or won't.

"Both marketing and sales are essential but the emphasis will often be higher in one direction or the other, marketing or sales, based on the way people perceive the importance of the decision.

"Remember this: In the New Economy thinking is moving further to the right in this diagram . . . towards thoughtful, rational decisions. That's why the circle with "New Economy Thinking" is on the right side of the chart. Here's why: When our resources are limited, people release them much more conscientiously.

"We were talking about Apple Computer earlier. The Apple Corporation has some of the most ingenious advertising (marketing) campaigns in the world. A simple logo tells a story that virtually anyone in the world can recite with common clarity. But have you ever been to their website or, better yet, an Apple Store?"

"As a matter of fact, just this weekend," the Frustrated Man answered.

"And what did you experience?"

"Even though the store was really crowded, the service was great. Two employees greeted me at the door and about six others smiled and offered help. This was before I got halfway into the store. I purchased something and one of the sales staff, in a distinctive blue shirt, took my order right there. I never even stepped up to a counter."

"And your impression?" the Visionary probed.

"Incredible. It was not only a productive encounter, it was just fun. I had someone demonstrate a new product and another took me to a displayed computer to show me how to address a problem I was having with my computer at home."

"That's sales," the Visionary said. "The moment relationships enter the equation you validate or invalidate every one of those branding messages.

"A friend of mine wrote a book where he asks the question, "What does Nike sell? Like Apple Computer, Nike has created a brand and it has created a perception in the minds of others. Here's how he stated it:

> "Nike sells athletic ability and victory. If you pay attention to Nike commercials, you will find that they don't talk about how long the laces last, the manufacturing of the soles, or the durability of the leather.
>
> "Instead, they emotionally connect to the deep drive we were created with to push past our limits to achieve something great. What you will see on Nike commercials is a group of kids in the street playing ball with a stick for the love of the game, a basketball player hitting a three on the buzzer to win the championship, or the look of determination on the early morning runner's face as she blazes through town.
>
> "The tangible product or service we all sell is the catalyst that addresses the deeper emotional need."[11]

"You want people talking about you. And you want them to be saying good things. If your branding message is powerful and if your marketing is strong, they will talk. But if you deliver what you say you will deliver, then they will say good things. All three are important – branding, marketing and sales."

---

[11] *Talkable*, 2010, by Guy Richards, pg. 36

"Branding and marketing gets you known, but sales and performance colors your reputation and, ultimately, determines if you will succeed."

"Charitable estate planning is a specialty field with which many attorneys and accountants are unfamiliar. There are some wonderfully creative ways in which people can increase their current income through estate planning and at the time of their death make substantial contributions. There are other exciting tools that make it possible for older constituents to make substantial gifts without incurring any loss in their current income. In fact, in some instances, these arrangements might increase it!."

"...there are two assumptions that we regularly make that are almost always wrong. The first of these is that when we say something, everybody understands what we just told them. The other is, that even if they did understand, you can't assume that anyone will expend the energy to deal with it!"

Chapter Fourteen

Painless Giving

Part of the frustration the Frustrated Man experienced was the continual need for financial support to sustain the work of his nonprofit. The time spent with the Visionary had caused him to think differently about how to accomplish his mission and his long-term plan included substantially reducing his dependence on donors.

Today the two were to meet at a local coffee café. This open and spacious facility was inviting and a favorite meeting spot for the entire community. The ambiance was casual, the service impeccable, and the unspoken message seemed to be, "Take a seat and stay awhile."

As they arrived and placed their coffee orders, they looked around the café. In one corner a group of students were huddled around a fireplace talking about something that appeared to be educational. A local businessman sat in a center table with his computer open, apparently checking email. About six moms had gathered in another corner in a circle with smaller preschoolers inside the circle playing with one another.

"I just love this place," the Visionary said. "Everyone comes here. It's clear they feel welcome. *It may have been marketing that brought people here but it's the sales reflected in how they treat customers that keeps them coming back.* A friend comes in here who is lactose intolerant. The staff discovered his condition and immediately left the store to purchase lactose-free milk for his lattes. They keep a gallon in their refrigerator just to accommodate him. Now is that service or not?"

"Wow," the Frustrated Man stated with amazement. "They actually did that? What does their brand say to you?"

The Visionary smiled. "Good question, my friend. It screams out service and caring. Sales and service reinforced the perception they were seeking to create. I tell everybody about this place and it's quickly developing a reputation."

Their drinks were delivered to them at the table. The attendant spoke to the Visionary by his first name, greeting him with a warm smile. He simply said, "Thanks, Christine. You're always so kind."

As they sipped their hot beverage the Frustrated Man began to discuss the entire matter of funding. He spoke of the changes he was making but affirmed his ongoing need for the financial involvement of others.

"You're doing a lot of things right," the Visionary said. "Years ago you introduced successful giving programs that have been effective in engaging the sustained financial involvement of many. Your Cornerstone 300 program is still the talk of the town and your special events still attract the 'Who's Who' in our city."

"You're right," the Frustrated Man reported, "and even with some of the declines we have experienced, people engaged in those programs continue to be the bedrock upon which we exist. Even those who have experienced financial losses in the current crisis, these core groups still stand with us doing what they can to make sure we succeed."

"That's wonderful, and that's what I would have expected. You've built a strong foundation."

"With your help, I might add," the Frustrated Man said, referring to another time ten years earlier in which he gained what he needed to survive and later flourish. "You gave me the tools and I simply acted upon them."[12]

"You built on core principles," the Visionary responded with a smile. "But times have changed as we both clearly know. There's less surplus and people are much more conscientious to preserve it. But that opens up new doors and I believe that the greatest opportunity in the New Economy for substantial giving is to be found in estate planning."

"While always a popular tool, it is taking on a new life in our times. It is estimated that over $60 trillion will be transferred from one generation to another in the next ten years. That's an enormous amount of money.

"Many of those individuals who will be making

---

[12] The events to which the Frustrated Man referred to can be reviewed in *Funding Your Vision: New Hope for Non-profits* (2000) by Gerald Twombly.

121

these transfers are being much more discretionary in the distribution of the assets they have accumulated. They're concerned about giving large sums of money at one time to their children realizing that a large influx of cash might be detrimental. They are engaging professionals to help them establish creative instruments that allow for the distribution of their estate over time to accommodate the various personalities of specific beneficiaries.

"But here's the main reason it is popular: Estate planning is painless giving."

"What do you mean?"

"A gift of one's estate will not be distributed, in most cases, until the death of the benefactor. In other words, he or she has total use of those assets throughout life. Giving you 10% of that estate is of little concern to the donor, since he or she won't need that money any more and family members have been cared for through some very creative estate planning tools.

"There's a truth you will soon discover," he added, "the older you get, the more concerned you are about leaving a legacy. And what better legacy could there be than to leave an endowed gift to an organization like yours that will be used for a new generation to sustain the important work you've begun."

"Interesting," the Frustrated Man said, "I know many people who would want to see our work continue. And they would probably be delighted to employ some type of estate planning tool to help us. But we haven't been very effective in getting this type of program off the ground."

"Your key donors may not know what options are available," the Visionary said. "Even if they did know about the options, that doesn't mean they will do anything.

"You see, there are two assumptions that we regularly make that are almost always wrong. The first of these is that when we say something, everybody understands what we just told them. The other is, that even if they did understand, you can't assume that anyone will expend the energy to deal with it!"

"I hear you," the Frustrated Man said. "So what does that mean I should do?"

"Provide them the tools they need. Offer them a packet that spells out how to go about making such a gift, and let them know you will provide them someone who can walk them through a process of evaluating what might be best for them. If you fail to do that it will be unlikely you'll see too many of these kinds of commitments."

"How extensive should that support be?" asked the Frustrated Man.

"As extensive as might be required. Charitable estate planning is a specialty field with which many attorneys and accountants are unfamiliar. There are wonderfully creative ways in which people can increase their current income through estate planning and at the time of their death make substantial contributions. There are other exciting tools that make it possible for older constituents to make substantial gifts without incurring any loss in their current income. *In fact, in some instances, these arrangements might increase it!* It's an amazingly creative discipline and given the fact that the numbers of seniors as a percentage of the total population continues to grow, it's an opportunity you cannot afford to miss."[13]

"I can see where that could make a huge difference for us," the Frustrated Man said. "We have some unbelievably committed current supporters and I'm guessing few if any of them have ever considered ways in which their interest in our work could continue beyond their lifetime."

"I'm sure that's true," agreed the Visionary, "and that's just one reason why you must consider making this part of your program."

---

[13] BGW Financial Services is a division of Building God's Way (www.bgwservices.com) and can provide full details of programs and services designed to enhance the work of nonprofits.

Christine came back to check on the two men. She brought a small dish of cookies with her. "I hope you have a phenomenal day," she said, and then she walked away.

"The Internet has become the tool of politicians and radicals, terrorists and evangelists, the searching and the seeking."

Chapter Fifteen

The Elephant in the Room

The Visionary started the next meeting with this, "When it comes to the New Economy, there's an elephant in the room. There's an obvious challenge that is not being properly addressed. It's the Internet, and, while many would prefer to ignore it, it impacts or will impact almost everything we do."

"Do you really believe that?" the Frustrated Man asked.

"Absolutely!" he responded with serious conviction. "It has revolutionized our world. Today you can check the best prices for anything you might want to purchase, gather insights from the greatest minds in the world through the blogs they publish, take courses for free from some of the world's foremost educators, research any topic that comes to your mind, store limitless amounts of data for virtually nothing, and even go on your personal safari of the earth, the moon, and other places while sitting in a chair in your office.

"You must harness the power of the Internet to survive in the New Economy. Through the Internet you can build relationships with your constituents, you can meet new people from around the world, you can communicate your vision though powerful video clips, you can receive contributions, and you can engage people in thousands of other ways."

"It certainly has become a part of our lives," the Frustrated Man pondered, "I've reconnected with long lost friends on social networking sites. My kids track their favorite athletes and musicians online. I have friends who do all their shopping online, other friends who play games online, and, regrettably, friends who are addicted to the worst that the Internet has to offer.

"As for my nonprofit, of course we have a website – which badly needs to be updated, and I check my email almost every day. Beyond that, I don't have much time for the Internet."

The Visionary nodded. "I understand, but I want you to think of it as a resource, a free tool that has been hand delivered to your front door that can be used in ways we cannot yet even imagine.

"A website and email are just the beginning of the thousands of possibilities that are unfolding for you. For example, many schools and colleges offer online courses. Many companies provide online teleconferencing for colleagues scattered around the world. Clubs meet online. I know of one church who has a weekly small group meeting online for individuals who travel extensively but still want the opportunity to study and spiritually grow together. Some families meet at a scheduled time each week because family members are scattered across the globe.

"The Internet is a meeting place that can be used to create community. It is rich place to harvest information, to track projects with partners anywhere, to pay your bills, to purchase and deliver your gifts, to share information with millions. And it's all accessible with a few clicks of the mouse.

"Internet radio, Internet television, and online videos cover every genre and topic.. The Internet has become the tool of politicians and radicals, terrorists and evangelists, the searching and the seeking. You buy books and read them, rent movies, buy groceries, and attend a seminar. You can promote your business and build a reputation. And you're often no more than a few keyboard strokes away from creating healing or hurt."

"What does this mean to me?" the Frustrated Man asked.

"It means that every issue relating to your organization's future needs to include a discussion on how you might be able to leverage the power of the Internet. Begin with the obvious: your website, interactive blogs, online board meetings, managing cohort groups, and the like. Your organization should have an ongoing task force constantly researching other ways to leverage this incredible tool."

"You're really serious about this, aren't you?" the Frustrated Man responding, not seeing this kind of intensity brought to many of their discussions.

"I was a slow learner," he responded. "On one hand I saw the power, but I also felt I was too old to learn. In the process I began to feel left behind, especially on the day when my adolescent grandson starting showing me things I never thought possible.

"There's a generation out there that is much more literate in terms of the possibilities of the Internet than you or I will ever be. Listen to them, talk to them, engage them as partners with you, and watch what happens.

"Stay on top of this. Better yet, engage partners who can keep you ahead of the curve. You don't want to finally begin using a web technology just when it's becoming passe and on it's way to obsolescence.

"The Internet is the future for much of what you will ever want to do. Harness it and you'll be able to do the unimaginable.

"Once you get past the shock of change, then you begin to adjust..."

"Education will see the greatest changes. The first to be hit will be private elementary and secondary schools to be quickly followed by smaller, private colleges."

"It's not that mega churches are bad, it's just that they may well end up a relic of the past in much the same way many of the cathedrals of Europe have become. Huge needs still exist but there might be better and much more effective ways to address them."

Chapter Sixteen

Winners and Losers

The sun was just rising as the Frustrated Man sat in his office, consumed with the project in front of him, and lost in his own world of thought and imagination.

Since his meetings with the Visionary he had made a special effort to think as a "New Economist." He began to look at issues from a different perspective. More and more, he found himself able to spot the difference between Old Economy and New Economy perspectives. Applying New Economy thinking to the challenges he faced liberated him. It opened his mind to endless possibilities. His conversations with the Visionary had given him permission to think differently, even radically. He loved the excitement of imagining again. It seemed that he had been unleashed and he felt an exhilarating freedom to move beyond his comfort level to do those things that he intuitively knew needed to be done. His confidence levels had grown and his frustration had diminished. It just felt good.

The silence was broken by the vibrating sound of the muted cell phone on his desk. He picked it up and looked at the caller identification. It was the Visionary and it was 6:15 am.

"My word," he answered, "aren't you the early bird this morning?"

"Early bird?" the exuberant voice exploded. "This is the best part of the day. I knew you would be up anyway so I figured this was the best time to get you!"

"I've had this hankering for a Pastrami Reuben and was wondering if we could meet for lunch at the corner deli. I'd like to share with you some thoughts I have on where I think the greatest changes will occur in the New Economy."

"Sounds great to me," the not so Frustrated Man responded. "How about 11:45. We just might beat the lunch crowd!"

The two met at the front door at precisely the same time. Together they walked to the front of the line, were directed to a table in the back of the room, and made their order before sitting down.

After exchanging pleasantries the Visionary began. "I've been doing a great deal of thinking over the last two years. I've been listening to those who have come to me. At the same time I've been watching trends, observing attitudes, and reading articles from every perspective on what will happen in the future.

"It's been interesting, to say the least. There are those who want to convince people that this is a short-term anomaly, an 'economic correction' that will quickly pass and life will go on as it was. Interestingly, their views are losing credence as time passes and they are not speaking so loudly these days.

"Now everyone seems to be coming to grips with the realization that change is taking place and some things will never be the same. Over the last several months I've jotted down some areas where I think the greatest changes will occur. And these changes will provide new opportunities."

The Frustrated Man interrupted, "It would seem to me that the greatest changes have occurred in how people perceive the times and how they have adapted to them in terms of their attitudes and outlook."

"You're right," he continued, "attitude and outlook are key. As I've shared before, people are afraid. Their fear has resulted in a more conservative attitude toward spending, saving, and priorities. What was important to them in the Old Economy holds little interest now. The trends are toward simplicity, community, caring, and family.

"I think this is wonderful! I'm having conversations with more people than ever before, I'm talking with my neighbors, playing games with my grandchildren, and enjoying backyard cookouts with friends. I'm driving a car with nearly 200,000 miles on it and don't plan to buy another until it drops; then I'll buy a used one.

"My point is this: I've made all those changes and I haven't lost my job. These are changes that I made because it became clear early on that these times were different. I'm happier and more optimistic that I've ever been."

"Well that's clear," the Frustrated Man laughed. "Frankly, I'm beginning to catch a little of that. What seemed overwhelming to me just a few short months ago seems exciting to me now. Go figure."

"Once you get past the shock of change, then you

begin to adjust," he replied. "Don't you find it interesting how quickly we can adapt? Once we get over the hump by accepting the new realities, we move on. Everyone can be resilient, it just takes some longer than others."

They both smiled. Soon the heaping sandwiches arrived. The oozing cheese and Thousand Island sauce dripping from the bread made eating their main priority for a few minutes.

"Well, here's the way I see it," the Visionary continued, wiping his hands on the wet napkin provided by their server. "There will be changes, major changes. Many of these will be driven by financial pragmatism. Other changes will be driven by the new attitudes that were caused by the crisis – everything from fear, to conservatism, to the need for community.

"Here are some examples. Car sales will continue to decline and probably will never reach earlier levels. Modern technology is simply capable of producing better cars that will run longer. The fear of debt and the vulnerability it creates will cause people to keep their cars longer, care for them better, and replace them with less expensive used vehicles."

"So it might not be a bad idea to invest in used car franchises," the Frustrated Man said.

"Well, maybe," he replied, smiling. "But that's not my point. My point is that the New Economy has facilitated change. Now it isn't quite as important to have a new car in the garage. When you get right down to it, everybody drives a used car. A shift in personal values has changed the culture.

"Education will see the greatest changes. The first to be hit will be private elementary and secondary schools to be quickly followed by smaller, private colleges. It might be perceived as prestigious to attend one of these schools but exorbitant tuition costs will drive people away. Enrollments will decrease and endowments will be drained. You'll see many closures."

"Does that mean the end of private education?" the Frustrated Man asked, "After all, many of the people who select these institutions are looking to them because they get something from them that's not available in the public sector."

"Agreed," the Visionary acknowledged. "The need for these institutions continues to exist. But the approach to running them is archaic and requires change."

"What do you think that change will look like?"

"It will undoubtedly include several things. The elephant in the room is the Internet. It can't be ignored and will be a primary player in education in the next decade. Online learning opportunities don't require the expensive overhead of maintaining a building, and, because geography is much less of a limitation, students can be recruited from a much larger pool. There will also be much more online competition among colleges as they try to bring their unique brand and distinctiveness to a new generation of learners.

"Students will continue to require one-on-one support. I think you'll see more secondary schools following a university model utilizing adjunct faculty, many traditional colleges will branch outside the campus to establish local community colleges that can be operated less expensively while still providing the educational focus unique to the sponsoring university. Cost will become a primary concern so outsourcing much of the instructional component through utilization of adjunct faculty begins to make good economic sense. This new model will also expand their market while still affording them the opportunity to maintain their distinctiveness. It's a much more affordable option for families who want something distinctive."

"Interesting," the Frustrated Man mumbled as he wrote rapidly on the legal pad on the table before him.

"This really isn't rocket science. This is common sense and it will prevail in the New Economy."

The server offered them a dessert menu. She recommended the cheesecake of the day and the Visionary nodded, ordering two.

He continued, "Colleges will change the delivery system making it possible for students to get baccalaureate degrees in three years. Student advising will rise to astounding new levels. The New Economy student is looking for a degree and the tools to be able to use it in a career. The college will take a much more active role in developing life-long relationships and support networks to help their graduates.

"Another big winner will be the private auxiliary services that will arise. Most public and private schools will be forced to jettison their athletic and arts programs. With financial cuts in the private sector and the threat of increasing tuition in private schools, costs will be seen as prohibitive. New Economy entrepreneurs will come in and fill the gap. This will occur in a number of creative ways. In some instances those services will simply be outsourced using already existing facilities; in other cases whole new comprehensive centers will appear in cities offering a wider range of programs that can be delivered on an *a la carte* basis. The consumer will rule."

"Interesting," the Frustrated Man said, "doesn't this kind of model exist in other places in the world?"

"Absolutely. It can be seen successful in practice in many places around the world. In Asia it has worked splendidly for years. Students go to school and then they participate in a wide range of options available to them after school is over. There are more options to learn about virtually anything that interests you."

"Fascinating! What other trends do you see?"

"Here's an important one: Bigger is no longer better. The trend will be toward smaller. In the Old Economy too much power was placed in the hands of too few people – whether in business or in government. When those people made bad decisions, we all reaped the aftermath of their poor choices. People will rebel against that in the New Economy. You will see larger businesses splitting up into smaller divisions, you will see community centers taking on a new life.

"Along with this, I think you will see a move away from mega churches and a move toward home churches. The very idea that larger congregations have huge facilities, means they often maintain very high debt. That doesn't make sense in the New Economy. If I'm being asked to give money to support a debt when I see people struggling all around me, my inclination will be to provide help where it is going to make the biggest difference. Most people don't feel very good about trying to pay someone else's debt when they struggle with their own."

"Yikes," the Frustrated Man breathed aloud.

The Visionary nodded. "It's not that mega churches are bad, it's just that they may well end up a relic of the past in much the same way many of the cathedrals of Europe have become. Huge needs still exist but there might be better and much more effective ways to address them."

"What do you mean?

"More churches are searching for ways to reach the non-traditional crowd by building multi-use community facilities that have the potential of generating income while still providing space for worship on Sunday.

"I know of one church that decided that they just didn't want to look like a church anymore. People weren't coming, especially the 40 and under crowd, so they chose to begin a network of coffee cafes that were opened throughout the week. Services for the community were held throughout the week and quickly they discovered that their impact and outreach was greater than ever before. They were reaching far more people. Most of their overhead was underwritten by coffee sales. And they were able to live a life of service that demonstrated the care that Jesus showed throughout His life and work. They even called themselves The Service Station[14] based on a verse in the Bible where Jesus said that He didn't come to be served but to serve.

"Expect to see a growing number of cottage industries. People are searching for independence and the New Economy is an entrepreneur's dream. People want a voice in those things that impact them and they will go to desperate ends to find it.

"Meanwhile, nonprofits will move toward building self-sufficiency. Their dependence on donors creates a vulnerability that most are finding unacceptable. Those who make grants, foundations and corporations, will look for ways to leverage their investments so every dollar has maximum impact. Individual donors will do the same.

"People are afraid of change. But change will happen, whether people want it or not. Every leader needs to ask the question, 'What am I to do? Preserve what is not working and die a slow death? Or undergo radical surgery in return for a healthy, productive, and fruitful life?' The answer, albeit unpleasant, is clear.

"A few years ago, Muhammad Yunus, the world's

---

[14] For more information regarding The Service Station go to: www.theservicestation.org and www.myservicestation.org.

leading social entrepreneur, founder of the revolutionary Grameen Bank, pioneer of microfinance, and winner of the 2006 Nobel Peace Prize--described his breed as '70 percent crazy.' It's extraordinary how often his fellow entrepreneurs have told us that they have been called crazy by the media, by colleagues, by friends, and even by family members. But they are crazy like the proverbial fox. They look for – and often find – solutions to insoluble problems in the unlikeliest places. They are driven by a passion to expand business thinking to reach people in need. Thus, many are pioneering and helping map out future markets where most of us would only see nightmarish problems and risk."

Crowds begin to arrive and many stood waiting for an empty table. The two rose to leave.

"The point that I'm making is this," the Visionary said, "change will occur. The winners will be those who spot the trends and act upon them. The losers will be those who will snooze away the opportunities only afforded a generation every 50-100 years. I've just shared a few; there are thousands more!"

Conclusion

You Snooze, You Lose

Two years later...

The Frustrated Man's organization had grown by over 200%, but his need for donations had dropped by 40%.

Much had changed. Seventy-five percent of the operating budget now came from monies generated by a seven different micro-businesses that were managed by their clients. Over 300 different individuals, young and old, were employed by these income-producing businesses. All four community service clubs were represented on the Community Advisory Board that was led by the city's mayor. The President's Council included the CEO's of businesses in the community. Churches had banded together in support of the organization's largest community outreach. Over $1 million had been deposited into the organization's endowment fund, all raised from estate gifts from long time organizational supporters.

Tonight was a special night. The man once known

as the Frustrated Man was to receive an award presented by the state's governor acknowledging him as the nonprofit Leader of the Decade.

Appendix

Nine Tsunamis that Will Rock Our World

The economic earthquake that has crippled many nations of the world has generated a series of tsunamis that continue to leave a swath of residual damage in areas far from the earthquake's epicenter. A single wave can create chaos; a series of successive ones will forever change the social and economic landscape.

My friend and business partner, Daniel Cook, has identified nine tsunami waves that will impact virtually every person, business, and organization in the world. It is Dan's opinion that every church, school, business and nonprofit must understand the impact off these tsunamis and implement a game plan with sustainable solutions in response.

1. **The Tsunami of Big Government** – The governments of the world continue to take on debt and are beginning to come to the realization that the payment of it will require limiting services or increasing income. Entitlement programs will continue to

consume the majority of national budgets and will spawn a dependence mentality that will crush personal initiative among a large segment of the world's population. In the United States the burden will fall on the same group of people that supply 80 - 90% of the giving to our church budgets and capital campaigns. As taxes go up, donations will go down.

2. **The Tsunami of the Millennial Generation** – The millennium generation (those born after 1988) is poised to assume leadership roles in society, business, and government. These predominantly "right-brain" thinkers will bring with them their ideas, values, and perspectives and will redefine business, organizations, and politics for the next century. Daniel H. Pink in his popular business book: *A Whole New Mind: Why Right-Brainers Will Rule the Future* predicts radical changes. This is the same group that is leaving the church in record numbers—some estimates show as many as 80% of this group have left the church and are not coming back. While they only make up 5% of the wage earners today, they will represent over 50% of the world's workforce within 8 years!

3. **The Tsunami of Tax Reform** – The massive debt incurred by governments portends inevitable increases in federal, state, and local taxes further reducing the expendable income generally devoted

for giving, investment, and purchasing. In addition we may very well see the deduction for 501(c)3 giving disappear within the next few years. Expect a long recovery from the worst financial crisis in 70 years.

4. **The Tsunami of Wealth Transfer** – Some $60 trillion dollars will be transferred from one generation to another in the next 40 years. This will fall into the hands of the Millennial Generation and its use will be guided by their set of values.

5. **The Tsunami of Inflation** – After a long period of minimal inflation and an unusually long recession and even slower recovery, inflation will eventually be essential to build vibrancy into a stagnant economy. Debtor governments will rely on inflation to reduce their debts to manageable levels. Increased costs will add increased financial burden to individuals and organizations who are seeking to build stability and predictability to cash flow.

6. **The Tsunami of Uncertainty** – The underlying attitude emerging out of the worldwide economic crisis is uncertainty. People are waiting for the last shoe to drop. This has created apprehension and a new financial conservatism that will result in businesses being slow to invest and donors being reluctant to give. The first wave of this tsunami has already hit.

7. **The Tsunami of Increased Nonprofit Activity** – Social needs have spawned a significant increase in the number of registered nonprofits and increased competitiveness for the charitable dollar. This phenomenon combined with the overall reduction in per capita giving spells danger for organizations dependent on contributions to maintain operational viability. Churches have gone from representing 80% of registered nonprofits to fewer than 6% in less than 15 years!

8. **The Tsunami of Education** – Some of the greatest losses in the last decade have come in the area of private education. Tuition dependence combined with reduced family income has resulted in catastrophic drops in enrollment and a larger number of private school closures. Many of the value-based educational alternatives once available in communities are being lost at every level (elementary, secondary, and baccalaureate).

9. **The Tsunami of Narcissism** – The underlying narcissistic culture has made it practically impossible for many individuals and organizations to see beyond their own needs to join together in community to resolve some of societies greatest challenges.

Dan is completing a book that not only gives expanded details of the impact to Christian organizations, it gives practical guidance as to solutions that can be implemented today to avoid the catastrophic consequences that could result from these tsunamis.

Resources

Please contact Jerry Twombly at:

Jerry@cdppro.com

for

- Interesting articles on current topics
- Order Jerry's latest published books including the best-selling *Funding Your Vision: New Hope for Non-Profits* and *Transforming Culture: The Church at Work in the World*.
- Free downloads of books written by Jerry
- Registration links for free online webinars
- Follow Jerry's speaking and teaching schedule throughout the world
- Learn about interesting new projects being initiated throughout the country
- Listen to Podcasts of training programs
- Discover how you can receive the professional certification designation, CDP (Certified Development Professional)

Jerry's personal outreach includes:

- Development Training and Certification Programs
- Funding Your Vision One-Day Seminars
- Adapting to the New Economy One-Day Seminar

Carpe Diem!

www.ingramcontent.com/pod-product-compliance
Lightning Source LLC
Chambersburg PA
CBHW070231180526
45158CB00001BA/382